PRAISE FOR *EDUCATION ACROSS BORDERS*

"*Education Across Borders* is a powerful cri de coeur, appeal, study, and manifesto from three fervently passionate, highly empathetic, and experienced educators who are transforming K–12 education for BIPOC and first-generation students, particularly from Haiti and the Dominican Republic. This book is a must-have for school administrators, teachers, and lawmakers, as well as parents and general readers. It is the kind of book that belongs in every classroom, as it could help safeguard young people's futures and even save their lives."

—EDWIDGE DANTICAT
author of *Brother, I'm Dying*

"*Education Across Borders* fiercely advocates that teachers of Haitian, Dominican, and other students with immigrant backgrounds—whose language and cultural needs are largely neglected in classrooms—must do better. Sylvain, Tamerat, and Cerat's collective years of teaching and research, and depth of theoretical knowledge, provide important insight for ensuring both academic success and positive socio-emotional development for students learning English. This book is for all who are deeply committed to the success of language-minority students and are willing to passionately advocate for it. As such, it should serve as a resource for every educator who teaches these students."

—AUDRA M. WATSON
director, WW Teaching Fellowship,
Institute for Citizens & Scholars

T0026423

"*Education Across Borders* is a marvelous gift. Brilliantly distilling an innovative pedagogical framework that allows teachers to center the needs of immigrant students, especially Haitians and Dominicans, in ways that are truly profound and revelatory. A must-read for all educators interested in transforming anti-racist theory into everyday classroom practice."

—PENIEL E. JOSEPH
author of *The Sword and the Shield:
The Revolutionary Lives of Malcolm X
and Martin Luther King Jr.*

"The four extended essays in this compelling book provide inspirational and pragmatic strategies to empower educators to turn their classrooms into spaces for transformative learning for their Haitian and Dominican students. A rallying cry recommended for all who care to connect their students to schools as sites of possibility."

—CAROLA SUÁREZ-OROZCO
cofounder, Re-Imagining Migration,
and Distinguished Professor,
University of Massachusetts, Boston

EDUCATION ACROSS BORDERS

IMMIGRATION, RACE, AND IDENTITY IN THE CLASSROOM

Patrick Sylvain,
Jalene Tamerat,
and
Marie Lily Cerat

Beacon Press, Boston

BEACON PRESS
Boston, Massachusetts
www.beacon.org

Beacon Press books
are published under the auspices of
the Unitarian Universalist Association of Congregations.

25 24 23 22   8 7 6 5 4 3 2 1

This book is printed on acid-free paper
that meets the uncoated paper ANSI/NISO
specifications for permanence as revised in 1992.

Text design by Michael Starkman
at Wilsted & Taylor Publishing Services

Library of Congress Cataloging-in-Publication Data

Names: Sylvain, Patrick, author. | Tamerat, Jalene, author. | Cerat, Marie
    Lily, author.
Title: Education across borders : immigration, race, and identity in the
    classroom / Patrick Sylvain, Jalene Tamerat, and Marie Lily Cerat.
Description: Boston, Massachusetts : Beacon Press, [2022] | Includes
    bibliographical references. | Summary: "A strong teacher development
    resource for white educators who serve BIPOC students and are looking
    for culturally relevant pedagogies that value the diverse experiences of
    their students" —Provided by publisher.
Identifiers: LCCN 2021034939 (print) | LCCN 2021034940 (ebook) |
    ISBN 9780807052808 (Trade Paperback : acid-free paper) |
    ISBN 9780807052815 (eBook)
Subjects: LCSH: Culturally relevant pedagogy—United States. | Critical
    pedagogy—United States. | Educational equalization—United States.
Classification: LCC LC1099.3 .S95 2022 (print) | LCC LC1099.3 (ebook) |
    DDC 379.2/60973—dc23/eng/20211104
LC record available at https://lccn.loc.gov/2021034939
LC ebook record available at https://lccn.loc.gov/2021034940

CONTENTS

Chapter 1

MY EDUCATIONAL WORLD

Democratic Pedagogy and Engaged Citizenry

Patrick Sylvain

Despite its nondemocratic society and underdeveloped institutions, Haiti has seen some great scholars and successful individuals graduate from various schools throughout the country, many of whom eventually went on to study abroad. Nonetheless, the educational curricula in Haiti were not engineered to meet the demands of the people they were meant to serve. Schools, in a traditional sense, have been institutional establishments where children grow and learn prescribed sets of instructions that are meant to measure accomplishments and mastery of skills. Such pedagogical modality, or conservative philosophy of education, is what John Dewey advocated against when he wrote:

> Since the subject-matter as well as the standards of proper conduct are handed down from the past, the attitude of pupils must, upon the whole, be one of docility, receptivity, and obedience. Books, especially textbooks, are the chief representatives of the lore and wisdom of the past, while teachers are the organs through which pupils are brought into effective connection with the

material. Teachers are the agents through which knowledge and skills are communicated and rules of conduct
enforced.[1]

This was the kind of educational world I experienced in
Haiti, and the kind of education my Haitian students as well
as the other international students I have taught were exposed
to. The uneven and stratified nature of the Haitian society
never provided equality of opportunity. Education, the suppos-
edly great equalizer, was a societal divergence. Another wedge
to further expose the contradictions within the society. To a
large extent, conservatively educated Haitians became ostensibly French, despite living in a place the French despised. The
encounter of a democratic classroom in the United States was
a shocking revolution. As Carola and Marcelo Suárez-Orozco
indicate in their coauthored book *Children of Immigration*,
classrooms "in the United States are dominated, however superficially, by an ethos of egalitarianism and democracy. The
immigrant child may initially come to experience the new social pace and structure as disorienting."[2] As in all revolutions,
there are side effects. In my experience, students who have depended on and needed the regimented structure have had difficulty functioning in the seemingly democratic environment
where educational punishments were not physical but rather
bureaucratic, and this eventually created structural pitfalls. It
took me a while to understand a large part of the American educational system, and then to eventually try to navigate my students away from the institutional pitfalls given my background
and experiences.

Throughout the world, the fundamental goal of education
is to teach students a certain predicted skill set that is aligned
with a national curriculum, or regional/district goals. Within
these fundamental goals for education, what differ are: (1) the

content; (2) the pedagogical approaches/methods; (3) who the society considers worthy to educate; and (4) the ways in which a particular society views children and their capacities. As US–based educators, we know that learning is constant, but what matters is the type of learning and the context in which that learning takes place. In the conventional "learning" context, the classroom, the relationships between teachers, students, content, and culture/community are key to understanding the dynamics of knowledge production.

In the context of American urban schools, which many immigrant students attend, notions of safety, achievement, and sometimes empowerment are central to the prospect of undoing centuries of denying access to education. In the Caribbean, in the time before independence for most of the countries, having an education was to have a privileged access to social mobility. Education was, and still is, among the institutions that best symbolize transcendence. Therefore, a school—and more particularly a classroom—is never regarded as a site for feeling good emotionally; rather, it is a site of strict knowledge production in order to attain an economic goal.

In the context of the West's conception of modern and progressive education, Jonathan Cohen reminds us of the history of the movement and situates the child at its center. He writes:

The notion that we can and need to understand the "whole child," including social and emotional functioning, was proposed and implemented in classrooms during the early part of the century by John Dewey, Felix Adler, and Maria Montessori. These pioneers of progressive education were soon joined by a growing number of students/teachers such as Anna Freud (who was first a teacher), Rudolf Steiner, and many others in Europe and the United States, all of whom sought to make educational curricula more relevant to the child's social and emotional experience. Progressive educators held that, optimally, we need to pay attention to *all* facets of the child; this includes an attempt to discover where each child's particular strengths and weakness lie, what the child's interests are, and which helpful (or unhelpful) coping strategies he or she has developed.[3]

These ideas or pedagogical philosophies tend to be fully embraced by most teachers and school districts in the United States. However, as we are interacting with a diverse population from various part of the world we need to be mindful of how we approach the notion of the "whole child" in relation to "emotional functioning." What may be a form of social and psychological engagement with a child may be perceived as prying from a person with a different cultural or pedagogical background where the totality of the child is not part of the pedagogical equation. In some cultures, the child's role is to go to school and learn. They are not to be heard from unless spoken to by the teacher, or unless they are propelled to ask questions relating to the material being taught. Additionally, the notion of creating dialogues between teachers and students simply does not exist if the student comes from a dictatorial or patriarchal space. Some Westerners developed philosophies as a result of the two world wars and other traumatic events that forced educators to examine those lived experiences in the context of education, but other parts of the world have not had the dialogic spaces or the psychoanalytical incentive or capacity to explore the whole being of the child within the context of learning in a democratic classroom.

I echo Steven Wolk's position when he asserts that "the idea behind the democratic classroom: [is] to create an environment of trust that allows children and their teachers the freedom to explore, to ask questions, to inquire, to think. If we want children—and later, adults—who can and will think for themselves, then we must have classrooms that allow them to do exactly that."[4] While this is indeed true, the problem arises with teachers who are not democratic, or who simply believe that certain students are not worthy of being treated democratically. Additionally, sometimes a school might also have teachers whose cultures never experienced democracy yet are expected or assumed to teach as if they already know what a democratic classroom looks like. Not only should school systems be mindful of their diverse and multilingual student body, but they should also be mindful of their diverse teachers' experiences and pedagogical philosophies.

I was born and raised as a Haitian, a proud one, with all of the values and the "burdens" that are associated with that identity. I grew up with doers, people who made an impact on the Haitian society, negatively or positively. I grew up firmly believing in the historical role Haiti played in making Blacks in the Atlantic proud. I grew up under a political dictatorship where President François Duvalier claimed he was the leader of the Black free world. Making use of the society's memory of the founding ancestors—Toussaint L'Ouverture and Jean-Jacques Dessalines, who gave us liberty—Duvalier injected his leadership alongside the national heroes by claiming he also enabled us to look white people in the eye without fear. However, I also grew up fearing the Tonton Macoutes, Duvalier's henchmen, who had the power to crush dissent and silence hopes. I grew up believing in education as the only earthly salvation. I grew up with books as gateways to the world, and as nutrients for the mind. I grew up learning to articulate my point of view and to be fearless while remaining respectful. I was raised in a way that I knew many other Haitian kids were not, but I did not know how privileged I was in receiving a richly democratic and civic outlook on life.

After I left Haiti and moved to Cambridge, Massachusetts, I began high school at Cambridge Rindge and Latin. As a student, I was made fun of because of my accent. I was made fun of because I was Haitian. Haitians were the butt of jokes in the 1980s due to the large number of boat people who were washing up on the shores of Miami, and the negative portrayal of Haitians as witchcraft practitioners.

To say that some of us were infuriated by the manner in which Haitians were treated at the high school would be an understatement. There were students who saw fighting as the only solution to garner respect. Others pretended they were Jamaicans in order to skirt the stigmas attached to being Haitian. Fortunately for us, we had a very progressive teacher, Mr. Monaks Kanel, who not only was an excellent math, health, and Haitian culture teacher who taught us how to read and write in Haitian "Creole," but he was also a politically conscious teacher who wanted us to be dynamic and dialectical in our thinking. It was in his classes that some of us were exposed to the various problems (illiteracy, overcrowded houses, work discriminations, identity issues, etc.) that Haitians were facing, and it was there that I learned the stories of two students who made it to the US by boat. Suddenly, the fact that I had migrated by plane and had a green card, or a permanent residency card, made me realize how fortunate and relatively secure I was in this country. I couldn't fathom the trauma those Haitians went through to find a safe passage to the United States. Being a refugee was not a laughing matter.

When I presented Mr. Kanel my idea of having a Haitian club at CRLS, he was instantly supportive and became an advisor to the club once its members were democratically voted into office. In 1984, I became the first president of the club and we made sure to have sophomores and juniors as assistant officers in order to have continuity. The Haitian club had a strong presence at CRLS, and as of 2019 it was still operational. What was crucial to me from Mr. Kanel's advice, besides his emphasis on the values of being a well-rounded educated person, was the fact that he believed in the youth as a source for a new generation of visionaries who could help in turning Haiti around. In my teaching and activism, I embody his aspirations. I remember how contentious the debates were among Haitian students when we were learning in Haitian "Creole." The older students who had been educated in Haiti believed that French was an inherently intellectual language and were vehemently opposed to the use of Haitian as a pedagogical tool. Slowly, some of the students changed their views when they saw how fluid learning became when those students who couldn't speak French freely participated in class discussions and the learning of new content became clearer and more cognitively accessible. My love and utilization of the Haitian language as a quintessential medium of communication and learning/teaching materialized in Mr. Kanel's class at CRLS.

In Cambridge, I became involved in Haitian local politics and social issues from a relatively young age, and perhaps one of my most prominent formative experiences occurred during my last year of college, when I worked as a teacher and counselor at a program for "at-risk" minority students in Cambridge: the Work Force. It was there that I learned about the prominent role and consequences of imposed stereotypes on the formulation of ethnic identity, as well as the psychological lacerations that resulted from being poor in an affluent city. A large number of the parents were functionally literate, the kids were on the cusp of dropping out, all of my students were on meal plans, and some of the parents were addicts. I came to

understand that after-school programs such as the Work Force
were necessary in alleviating certain problems, but they ultimately became temporary bureaucratic fixes when educational
institutions' failures vis-à-vis minorities, and Black people in
particular, were not addressed. The dysfunction of some of the
parents wasn't simply a series of individualized problems; they
were systemic and symptomatic of a nation that refused to fully
address the foundational problems of racism in the context of
a technologically advanced capitalistic society, which relied at
first on slavery and then ultimately on forms of structural discrimination and repression for the benefit of the status quo.

The housing projects within which the Work Force op-
erated became a part of the stepped-up measures the City of
Cambridge provided to overcome the institutional failures,
although the institutions themselves were never scrutinized as
possible culprits. With my students, I explored issues of zoning,
the politics of housing projects, and property ownership. We
even discussed the politics of collateral punishment relating to
drug possession on housing projects' grounds. With the federal
government's War on Drugs in full effect, several of my students had family members or close friends whose entire families
were forced to vacate their homes because drugs were found
in their apartments. Regardless of the infractions, the punishment was severe and lives were disrupted in ways the system
did not concern itself with. The victims became numbers and
the dysfunctional policies had real consequences. I wanted my
students to understand they were not the projects; they simply lived in housing projects, and the places they lived were
far better than most Third World houses. I wanted them to
think of transition, a place that might help them attain their
dreams. There was a way out. It was there that I learned not
to adopt prejudices against African Americans as many other
immigrants have done and are still doing. It is easy to scapegoat

African Americans when one has been bombarded by negative representation of African Americans even before arriving in the United States. It is easy to further demonize a group that is already demonized by the mainstream society, a group whose history is suppressed or at least dismissed. It was hard for me to embrace the reality that American society, which professes to be democratic and just, does not care about educating all of its citizens. I had to always make parallels to Haiti with some of my students' conservative Haitian parents who did not want their children to be associated with African Americans. I wanted for those parents to seriously think about trenchant class and color prejudices in Haiti, and to link them to the rigid caste and penal system in the United States. What kind of society would rather spend more money on prisons than on educating its disadvantaged population? I would ask them to ponder that. During the Ebonics debate, I would draw parallels between French and Haitian "Creole" to shed light on the notion of language community and linguistic socialization. Here I am thinking of Theresa Perry who suggests that: "Black language is largely an uncontested area of Black shame."[5] Black immigrants' distancing themselves from African Americans is not only due to a lack of historical understanding, but it also has to do with avoiding shame and claiming exceptionality through a politics of differentiation. Certainly, the notion of divide and conquer plays a very important role when one group is viewed more favorably than another by the economically dominant group. However, as Theresa Perry argues, "while being a Black immigrant might advantage one in a relationship to African Americans, the marker of skin color and what it represents in the white imagination inevitably cancels out some, but clearly not all, of the benefits that accrue from being an immigrant."[6] I understood the capacity of the American system (local, state, and federal) in addressing, as well as redressing, certain issues that have historically been divisive. Dismantling structural racism was never a priority, and the educational institutions— even in a purportedly liberal city like Cambridge—continue to shortchange minorities. Unfortunately, and although I received full permission for my outings, my contract was not renewed after I took several students on a comparative zoning trip to a few nearby suburbs. The director claimed a lack of funding, although we had actually received a large grant to enlarge the scope of the program. I assumed I was too political and not a conventional gatekeeper.

After college, when I became a history and English as a Second Language teacher for the City of Cambridge, working predominantly with Haitian students, I was able to recognize many of the same issues, and began my informal work as an ethnographer by systematically gathering data and learning from my students' lives. I became curious about existing patterns in values, beliefs, and experiences, and how they correlate to actions.

By the time I was hired to become a middle school teacher in the Cambridge Public Schools, I was already published and prepared to encounter those Haitian students who were deemed illiterate, as well as low skill English-language learners who had to be prepared, in three years or less, for high school.

During my first year of teaching, self-elevation through knowledge was my guiding principle. The first eleven Haitian students that I taught at Robert Kennedy Elementary in East Cambridge consisted of seven girls and four boys who ranged from eleven to thirteen years of age, among whom were two Jehovah's Witnesses, five Catholics, and four Baptists. However, I knew the parents of five of the eleven students were secret Vodou practitioners. All of the students were aware that I knew a lot of their parents' secrets or "peculiar" living conditions. They also knew that I considered my knowledge a privilege and

I wouldn't expose their lived "contradictions." To further complicate matters, one student was illiterate, three were functionally literate, four were fully functioning at the fifth grade level although they were placed in the seventh grade, and the other three were at relative grade level and simply needed to learn English to be able to transition into the mainstream once they got to high school. As a result, right away I established a culture of trust and of a pedagogical *koumbit* where the students who were at grade level would be the group leaders of three distinct groups that I had formed, and their tasks were to function as kinship clusters where every single member must succeed. I taught each group leader how to teach, in the broad sense, and they were rewarded with extra points. All of the student leaders were female and all of them, in their adult lives, became professionals. Two of them, NS and PS, became teachers and the other, AT, went into business. The student who was illiterate, PJP, learned how to read and went on to Cambridge Rindge and Latin to further his remedial education, and after graduating from high school he became an electrician.

I mention the religious affiliation of my students for the reason that, in general, religion is still a very important personal and sociocultural wedge for Haitians. Families can be divided along religious beliefs. Most Haitians are very upfront and proud of their Christian faith in the same way that they can be very proud and even boastful about their ability to speak French. Inversely, for the most part, the very same Haitians who are forthcoming about their belief in Christianity tend to be very secretive about their belief in, and, or, practices of Vodou as their ancestral and familial religion. As such, I kept arguments about religion away from the classroom and only addressed religious issues or beliefs when they broached the scientific realm, and therefore arguments based on logic and scientific facts were allowed without discarding their religious beliefs. For example, my students' beliefs about women being weaker and necessarily submissive to men were completely eradicated in my class. Another belief, that they had heard of people transforming into werewolves, cows, and other animals, was also deconstructed and dismantled. In other words, cultural or religious myths had to be scientifically proven or logically explained without leaving any doubts. Although young, I demanded rational thoughts from them and not hearsay. Over time, I also noticed a proportionate reduction in gossip. However, during the last period on Fridays when they were allowed to be creative through their storytelling, no limits were imposed on them except for the exclusion of violent and vulgar language. Even during storytelling, I required confident postures, engagement with the public, and efficacious articulation. Every activity was geared toward self-elevation. I feared for my students in the face of the consumptive trappings of the United States, where products are linked to identity formation, taking into account how seductive material objects—the "bling"—can be for children who came from poor countries and are trying to assimilate in various ways where consumerism is woven into the local culture. I wanted for them to remain connected to schools as a site of possibilities and not a depot of frustration, or a dropout arena. As such, I am reminded of Geoffrey Canada's remarks that for "millions of teenagers growing up in America, school is something that they feel only marginally connected to. To them schoolwork seems disconnected from their lives. They complain that it's boring and find it irrelevant."[7] As an immigrant—regardless of the racism and the hardship—school remains relevant, and I made sure my students believed that and pursued their goals.

Self-elevation through knowledge, a part of my original philosophy of education, is an acquired condition based on the development or reinforcement of an inquisitive personality who seeks to feel or is capable of feeling and understanding innate human suffering. Again, as a hybrid pragmatic idealist who is informed by the Haitian notion of *koumbit,* I approached education as a road not only to self-elevation but to self-revolution. It was not an easy road for me, and it certainly was a difficult road for many of my students who had to battle with family demons and self-contradictions and faced self-hate.

My students who knew how to read and were fortunate enough to go to good schools had to reflect on the sacrifices their parents made, and they had to ponder on the kids their age who lived in the same neighborhood but either did not go to school or attended mediocre schools. My conversations with them concerning the students who did not know how to read required of them to reflect on their own family members who did not know how to read, and how they felt about it. It required of them to think of education as a basic human right, and of the multitude of rights violated in Haiti due to the extremely high rate of illiteracy. It also required of them to think of how privileged they were to be in the United States and to take advantage of everything positive this country offered them. I also required each and every one of them to have a library card. The road to self-elevation and to self-revolution began with a sincere introspection, with an earnest evaluation of the immediate environment and the position of the self in relation to their dreams and aspirations. Our conversations were, in a sense, intense and disciplined with a practice of trust and respect. My students knew that my philosophy was guided by a respect and love for human life and the betterment of the human condition. They knew that I cared for their well-being as they searched for their individual selves in that new strange and vast land that can be dizzying at times. They also knew that I expected of them to embrace the truths of their existence without expecting to materialize those truths as permanent conditions of who they are or will be. They knew they were capable of self-elevation and self-revolution as long as they were disciplined and patient enough to transcend their material and spiritual conditions. In a sense, I wanted them to embrace the opportunities offered by the United States to become the people they envisioned themselves to be, or at least to start thinking about their future in a different way.

When I think of Robert L. Fried's book *The Passionate Teacher*, I know he was indirectly addressing teachers like me who understand the demands of educating children from a place of social equilibrium, and from social justice perspectives instead of a bureaucratic checklist of formula-based pedagogy that does not address their environment:

> Our society's economic and social traumas are familiar to all of us, as is the range of special needs students bring with them when they come to school. Teachers who work in schools within neighborhoods plagued by poverty, violence, and family hardship face much greater obstacles in trying to create the right environment for learning.[8]

I began teaching the year the Haitian military—supported by the US State Department, the White House, and the US Embassy in Haiti—led a coup d'état against Jean-Bertrand Aristide, a democratically elected president. Some of my students witnessed dead bodies in the streets and heard the ringing machine gun shots; one of them saw her father dragged into the streets, savagely beaten, and then set ablaze. I began teaching students whose parents had never heard of the concept of democracy until 1986, some of whom certainly voted for the first time in their lives in 1990. Additionally, some of my students had never seen a modern and fully organized city until they arrived in Cambridge. I knew I had to introduce them to the bureaucratic democracy of the United States, the sociocultural etiquettes, and the eventual racism they would be facing. Most importantly, I had to pre-boost their self-confidence before their eventual encounters with anti-Haitian sentiments and Negrophobia.

I was fortunate to have been fully supported by former Cambridge Public Schools Superintendent Mary-Lou McGrath and the then-principal of the Robert Kennedy, Mrs. Mroz, who provided funding in order to conduct field teaching/research with my students. That included visiting Italian restaurants and centers so that we could learn about Italy. The same was true when we did a unit on China. The students learned to eat with chopsticks and prepared reports on their excursions. We went to museums, universities, and libraries. When PJP learned how to express himself in English and was also able to write his first full and complete paragraph in Haitian and then in English, we went for ice cream. Education was not just about subject learning, but about undoing traumas, overcoming fears and inadequacies. For me, education is about establishing a relative social equilibrium in a child's potential toward self-elevation. Self-love, self-acceptance, and learning to read the world while reading the word, as Paulo Freire expressed it, was (is) also my vision. Education still is to me a true democratic endeavor and process that begins with critically reading the world:

> For this reason also, as I have said so many times, *teaching* cannot be a process of transference of knowledge from the one teaching to the learner. This is the mechanical transference from which results machinelike memorization, which I have already criticized. Critical study

correlates with teaching that is critical, which necessarily demands a critical way of comprehending and of realizing the reading of the word and that of the world, the reading of text and of context.[9]

As Haiti was once more mired in political violence, I witnessed the toll it had taken on young teenagers. The distrust, anger, and shame they displayed. Also, some of the parents couldn't understand why their children were so angry at the people they loved, and why some of them swore they would never return to Haiti. I understood them. As the country became exposed to the world and was labeled an international basket case, and more desperate people fled the country by boat, I knew that I had to prepare myself pedagogically to prevent further divisiveness among my students who were newcomers to the city. I found material that reinforced self-love, stories about other places like Vietnam and countries in Latin America, where people endured civil war and labor hardships and migrated to the United States illegally. They had to understand the world in the context of slavery, conquest, exploitation, military occupation, and dictatorship. But we also learned about hope and determination through the stories of the Jews who experienced Germany's concentration camps. They learned about the Japanese internment camps in the United States, and they also learned about the ongoing trials and tribulations of African Americans. All the while I reinforced the need to achieve a higher education in order to have choices in life. Every month I had a new student.

Over the years of teaching immigrant children, particularly Haitians, I've come to realize that instruction, or traditional school education, is not at all sufficient for children or people who have been oppressed; their education must be supplemented in order to cultivate their individual abilities. I saw my role as an educator and not simply as a teacher of subjects. An educator is a holistic pedagogue, one who can awaken talents, foster dreams, push for meaningful characteristics of each pupil to be applied to practical as well as to life-situational circumstances. I am reminded of a passage in Jonathan Kozol's book *On Being a Teacher*: "[The] hidden curriculum, as we have seen before, is the teacher's own integrity and lived conviction."[10] It was absolutely crucial for me to break away from Haiti's traditional pedagogy of the distant authoritarian teacher. This was a new moment for me as well as for the students to embrace a new pedagogical journey with high expectations, patience, determination, and caring. Since growing up in Haiti and later on in high school, I was becoming cognizant of the weight of society on those labeled poor and illiterate. After college, with the various sociopolitical studies and psychosocial experiments that I had learned about, I knew that the institutional failures of Haiti coupled with the structural racism against African Americans would be a toxic mix for my Haitian students who were poor, Black, and foreign. In the context of racial inequality and the hidden cost of being Black in the United States, I did not want them to buy in to various studies that claimed Blacks performed worse than whites when looking at the achievement gap, that students with uneducated parents are more than likely to drop out of school or to never attend college, and that French was a language of knowledge.[11] Those broad and categorical reports and studies would ultimately become self-fulfilling prophecies if they went unchallenged and uncontextualized. Everything had to be examined and we had to find examples to prove those broad reports wrong. Many of my students knew of someone who went to university as a first in their respective families, or who were attending a university while their parents worked as nurses' aides, taxi drivers, and custodians. Self-determination, discipline, and a passion for learning were my guiding principles for my students. I knew that an excellent classroom was one that engaged students and would therefore be beneficial, as Suárez-Orozco's research indicates:

> When an immigrant child finally sits at her desk in her new classroom, a world of possibilities can open. In some classrooms, immigrant children will flourish. During the course of our fieldwork, we have observed classrooms where teachers constructively engage their students' energies, optimism, and willingness to work hard. Children in these classrooms are surrounded by peers who recognize and support the crucial role of school in their future well-being. They are exposed to a curriculum that presents meaningful ideas in critical ways, and they have access to instructional technologies and other up-to-date classroom materials.[12]

I wanted for my students to believe they could beat the odds if they were willing to make sacrifices. I made sure they knew and understood that intelligence (also intellect) was not the domain of any one race or nation, that learning was about passion, a willingness to transcend boundaries, and feeding one's deep craving to accomplish big dreams without taking shortcuts.

The ills of Haiti had to be tossed out (dictatorship, classism, pseudo-aristocracy) while we kept the beauties (orientation toward family and education, hard work, humor). The same was true for the ills and beauties of the United States. I paid particularly close attention to the pragmatic side, which is a societal quality that I believed Haiti and Haitians would benefit from, since Haitians are hampered by the old French aristocratic mentality that has created a major chasm through the society, and which includes prejudices vis-à-vis the Haitian language that all Haitians speak.

LEWENBERG

After I left the Cambridge Public Schools and assumed my new position as an ESL/History teacher at a middle school in Boston, I did not know the extent to which the cultures of the Boston Public Schools were so vastly different than those of Cambridge. To begin with, the Cambridge school system is smaller and much more affluent in comparison to the various Boston neighborhood schools operating in neighborhoods that had experienced major "white flight" during the 1970s and that slowly became "working class" or "immigrant" schools. The Solomon Lewenberg Middle School was such a school, the quintessential urban school that had shown promise when it first served the large Jewish population of Mattapan during the mid-1920s to the early 1940s, and then a mainly white Irish Catholic middle class until the early part of the 1970s.

When busing, school desegregation, and the economic crisis of the late 1970s hit Boston, the Lewenberg was directly affected and it became known as the "Looneyberg" due to the amount of trash, fights, and other disruptions that occurred there, preventing the normal business of the school to take place; of course, its reputation plummeted and the nickname remained. Although things had somewhat changed in the 1990s, by the time I arrived there in September of 1998, the cynical old-timers welcomed me to the "Looneyberg," although I had no clue what they were referring to. I later found out the challenges of the school and the pockets of difficulties some of the teachers faced. However, the principal, Mrs. Mayfield, was a very supportive and fair administrator who was dealing with all the possible cards in her deck. The teachers seemed divided along color, class, and nationality lines. Even the Haitian teachers were divided into two camps: those who were French speakers and educated in Port-au-Prince versus those who were raised and educated outside the capital city and preferred to communicate in Haitian or in English.

As the language specialist, my job was to get to know the students and to assess their overall skills so the school would have a holistic picture of each child. What I did not anticipate was the subculture of animosity that existed among the bilingual teachers. I walked into a venomous pit. During our first official meeting, we were nine teachers in the room (four women and five men) and besides telling me their names and the subjects they taught, no one spoke for a good half an hour. I spoke to fill the void and eventually to dismiss the meeting. Ultimately, Mrs. Mayfield had to attend the next meeting, where she demanded the full cooperation of the staff to finally get the ball rolling. Within six months of my leadership, the teachers were talking and even superficially joking with one another. However, prior to getting to that point I was warned by one of the teachers, Mr. P., that I had to dance on one foot just like everyone else. To his surprise, I calmly responded that I was fully functional and happy being bipedal and that *monopedality* was hazardous.

Besides the usual love relations (or affairs) that went sour among some of the staff and therefore created rivalries, the Haitian teachers were divided along class and color lines. It could have been coincidental, but the lighter-skinned and French-speaking Haitians formed one camp and the darker ones formed another group. It seemed to me that a large part of the conflicts among Haitian teachers in the school arose out of old habits of interactions, misreadings, and miscommunications, including body language. Unfortunately, gossip and personal susceptibilities did not help in alleviating tensions. The ills of Haiti were reproduced at the school and I had to navigate the divisive murky water where the children's futures were on the line. It was like pulling teeth, and I had arguments with a couple of teachers, but one by one I formed alliances until we could fully work together without backstabbing. Collegiality and professionalism were my basic approach, and I knew sooner or later they had to give in. Regardless of how frustrated I was, my expectations were fairly high and just. I wanted to have cohesion among the bilingual staff so the students wouldn't be defenseless. There were a few teachers who held anti-immigrant views, and I made certain that the students, while in the cafeteria, hallways, library, and the gym, were fully on their best behavior so they wouldn't be scapegoated. In a way, the students learned to police themselves and earned points that accrued toward their eligibility for school field trips and other nonmandatory school-wide or cluster-based activities. One thing I've learned over the years is that, as we are all social beings, even the worst student does not want to be left out.

Regarding the teachers, unfortunately, we had a couple of slackers: old-timers who were more babysitters than teachers and had to modify their behavior only when the students' twice yearly assessments came around, and their promotion to the next grade after each school year was based on measurable numbers and not just the teacher's whimsical desires. We had to have a process—a fair and measurable one. Not one teacher could decide a student's promotion. We worked in a cluster, and within it, we had created sub-clusters (language/math and science, literacy and special education). Each sub-cluster had three teachers and two of the teachers had to be in solid agreement or disagreement regarding a student's placement. We also included counselors as well as the school psychologist as part of the dialogue. Additionally, each student had a portfolio. The teachers who were doing their jobs were on top of it and complied; those who were not, however, felt burdened and complained of having to do extra work. So, folders with the students' names were provided and the teachers simply had to place copies of the corrected works in each student's folders. Eventually, everyone came on board.

The Lewenberg was a life-changing experience for me, and I came into contact with Haitians of different socioeconomic layers who presented diverse sets of problems. Problems that varied not only in degree but also in the circumstances from which they arose; these circumstances differed tremendously than those of the Haitian families who lived in Cambridge. For one thing, Cambridge's smaller size and the available social agencies perhaps contributed to the alleviation of certain problems. However, most importantly, more nuclear families seemed to live together in Cambridge, instead of the family arrangements made up of "aunties," "cousins," or "good friends" that I witnessed in Boston. The common factors, however, were the children who were being reunited with family members they had not really physically known while they were growing up in Haiti, and such factors presented their own conundrums.

It was at the Lewenberg that I met seventh graders who were already in gangs and others who were being pressured to join. It was also there that I witnessed the negative pressures the Haitian identity bore and how concealment of that identity was a matter of survival for many. As a form of survival mechanism, some students Americanized themselves rather quickly in a matter of style, like accent and fashion, rather than substance. Therefore, we had an extremely high incidence of students who spoke English well but couldn't read properly. Those students, a handful of whom happened to be girls, were the most disruptive. Upon my arrival, I can only assume that the staff, unaware of my background and thinking they could pass on their problems, had assigned some of the worst-behaving students with the most acute literacy complications to my classes. It was then that I knew the students were being moved around without having a properly administered assessment and diagnosis. One of the girls, S, had repeated the sixth grade and was on track to repeat the seventh. She spoke English relatively well. After a few weeks in my class, I discovered that S had been in the US since she was nine years old and not one teacher discovered that she was functionally literate and was having issues at home. Some of the students' literacy-related issues were camouflaged by behavioral complications that were also rooted in difficult home arrangements. S was the family's babysitter for her four siblings; S was also the interpreter as well as the occasional cook. In addition, S had to hang with her female crew. A group of Americanized Haitian girls who swore not to ever get beaten up by African Americans, and therefore were fronting their own toughness in order to earn respect. With a concerted effort, S learned how to read and called me "Pops." After S finished reading her first book in class during the eighth grade, she screamed: "I can read, I can read. Pops, I did it." She hugged me and we cried that day and a few of the other students also cried. By the time she graduated S had transformed and become a model student and naturally put all of the girls in line. Even some of the boys, fortunately, followed her leadership. A leadership she had earned, a leadership we had turned into a positive asset.

I encountered other issues at the Lewenberg, one that was so grossly violent I would have to write a chapter or even a book to explain it all. It was a case that involved multiple agencies, and I eventually appeared in front of a grand jury as a key witness. That case had a direct link to the authoritarian history of Haiti, and the fact that some families never considered children as autonomous beings with personal rights. It was a case that involved severe psychological manipulations masterminded by a psychopath who happened to be a former member of the defunct Haitian military. That case shook my core as a human being and made me even more committed as a teacher.

The authoritarian culture ran so deep within the Haitian culture that I even had a parent who brought a whip (a twisted cowhide that was used during slavery) for me from Haiti to use against her child, or any other child for that matter, if she were to ever be disobedient. To this parent's surprise, I informed her that it was illegal to beat children in this country and, furthermore, I was against corporal punishment. In any event, she told me that the whip was the "mister" at her house and she was not going to let her child be a vagabond in this country. I said okay, but I emphasized that communication was important and tough love could also do the trick. It was after the parent left that some of the students informed me that one of the teachers used some of the Haitian modes of punishment, including having students stand in a corner while facing the wall, as well as kneeling down for a period of time. I was furious. Without having proof, I couldn't raise the issue up with any one teacher. However, as a part of a larger conversation, I raised the issue of the "war against children of color" that Dr. Peter R. Breggin detailed in the book he coauthored with Ginger Ross Breggin to promote awareness about various forms of violence inner city youths faced as well as the concerted effort to "scientifically" control people of color in the United States.

I remember Mr. P and Mr. M heaving when I talked about the outdated modes of discipline that Haitians used in the schools. With all seriousness, Mr. P looked at me and said: "What you are doing with the students is dangerous, this democracy thing is not for us. We are used to order, and a good whipping is sometimes good. You're only one person, you can't spread democracy. What about when you're gone?" I had learned to talk to Mr. P, whom I grew to appreciate because he was willing to speak on behalf of those who did not want to confront me, and so I pulled Breggin's book from my bag and read a passage to him:

When women, children, racial minorities, or the poor are oppressed, their leadership must encourage a commitment to personal responsibility as well as social activism. But for those of us who are more advantaged, our responsibility lies in helping to lift the burden of prejudice and inequality off their backs. Justice requires, first and foremost, that we take responsibility for our contribution to the problem. If, instead, we focus our attention on the personal responsibility of the victims, we deny our own role in allowing the oppression to persist, and heap injustice upon injustice.[13]

Mr. P smiled and said to me that "injustice is all around." I agreed with him, and I proceeded to ask him if I could read one more quote. He agreed, and I began by changing the pronoun to the collective *we*: "[We need] to shed the old values that impede progress, and to develop a new set of more positive ideals based on empathy for all citizens and especially for children of all races and economic status."[14] By the time we were done talking, he realized that I was steadfast in my belief in creating an environment where the students would strive and be respected while respecting themselves.

It wasn't until 2000 that the old animosity had dissolved and class distinctions were put aside when everyone saw the benefits of working together for the interest of the students. The Haitian students had the highest math scores at the school (and also ranked among the highest in the district). The students in the literacy program had received the support they needed, and their progress was properly monitored when they made the transition to the regular bilingual program. Finally, the bilingual students were also monitored as they partially or fully transitioned into the mainstream general education program. We had an absolutely functional and cohesive bilingual program

that became a model for the Boston school system, to the point
that Mrs. Mayfield wanted me to pursue my principal certifica-
tion. I was flattered, but I was never interested in becoming an
administrator. I was at home in the classroom, and the changes
in the students' behaviors, attitudes, and inter-relations were
profound. As for the staff, the end-of-the-year picnic that I
organized became a major point of cohesion, and every single
member wished that we had had such solidarity earlier. Unfortunately, in June of 2003, with the dismantling of bilingual
education and other policy changes that affected the program,
many of us were transferred to other schools.

NBPMS

In September of 2003, having been recruited to teach at the
newly built New Boston Pilot Middle School, I felt relief when
I attended the first full staff meeting and then one at my assigned academy. The teachers sat together, joked with one another, and seemed to form an instant bond as if they were a
new breed of pedagogical warriors ready to battle negativity. I
saw teachers and administrators who had taught in Cambridge,
as well as former classmates of mine and new graduates from
Harvard. Additionally, I was glad that the school required uni-
forms and each academy was equipped with its own computer
lab as well as a modern science lab. The school had a large dance
studio, a modern music room with brand new equipment, and
a full-size gymnasium. Furthermore, the staff was genuinely
cheerful about teaching there. The teachers and staff members
looked professional. I was beyond optimistic. Besides, I was going to work with Spanish-speaking students and I thought it
was going to be a wonderful opportunity for me to not only
brush up on my Spanish but also to have a positive impact
on the mainly Dominican and Puerto Rican student body. Indeed, the first week, although we worked long hours, was elec-

trifying. It really did feel like a new school, a new culture, a new way of being in a system that had pockets of success. We were going to show Boston how the pilot model was the future.

By the third week, the polished students, the well-groomed staff, the aura of optimism, and the order that reigned throughout the school started to dissipate. Suddenly, some teachers started to complain about being tired and afraid that the school was about to implode. I kept my optimism because our academy was doing well, despite a few kids who started to test the order and the united front that we maintained. By the last week of September, all four of the academies were in panic mode. Fights had broken out, in-school suspensions were up, Boston police patrol cars were seen out front, and the intercom was abuzz with calls for the security officers. Something was wrong. Apparently, many of the district schools had sent their most problematic students to NBPMS and the school was simply too big to manage teenagers with preexisting problems.

In any event, when it came to my classroom, that's where I felt the heartache. As a veteran teacher with a solid track record, I thought I was ready to handle almost anything given my exposure to the world. When my Spanish-speaking students, mainly Dominicans, decided not to speak English and insisted that I understood enough Spanish to conduct my classes in their language, I was puzzled. I was aware of forms of linguistic resistance, and I had had a few students in the past who initially refused to learn English and eventually gave in. But when an entire class was held hostage by a handful of students who had behavioral as well as literacy issues, that complicated matters. What made it worse: one of the boys (JP) who was the ringleader, was a seventh grader who was extremely vocal, funny, and also violent; he disliked Haitians or, at least, was proud to have witnessed as well as participated in the beatings of Haitians in his region of the Dominican Republic. JP was from the countryside and dreamed only of playing professional baseball, which he was apparently very good at. I later found out that he had an awful relationship with his dad, who had very little schooling but dreamed for his kids to be somebody in life. JP was the youngest and was not really raised by the father, who had been living in the States. JP was not at all interested in school, and was also of the opinion that he didn't need to speak English well to survive.

My real nightmare started in mid-October, when my class gained a new member: a Spanish-speaking student who spoke English well but could not function in the mainstream classes and was therefore deemed an English as Second Language learner for the fact that he was Puerto Rican. This student, DJR, was given the moniker "Chucky" because of his small size and his horrible attitude. When DJR came to my class, he was happy to get to speak Spanish, be a class clown along with JP, and also push for a no-English movement. To speak English was to be a gringo, and most of them didn't want to be considered gringos. I felt powerless and overwhelmed.

After nearly two months of being unable to cover three weeks' worth of lessons, and some of the girls starting to want only to sing popular bachata songs in the class, I lost it. I walked out of my classroom and cried. When the students realized what they had done, those who had stayed silent became concerned and complained to the other "bilingual" teacher, Dr. A, who happened to be Dominican and was furious with them. Two days passed with minor incidents, but the overall refusal to learn English was still present. Seeing no way out, I wrote my first ever resignation later. My academy leader was shocked and intervened. He begged me not to quit and we searched for the best possible solution.

When the students discovered that I was about to quit due to their lack of desire to learn, and saw how hurt I was by the fact that they were throwing away their future, they came to the realization that I cared, and that JP as well as DJR were a major part of the problem. For about a week, Dr. A and I combined our classes and taught our respective subjects so that the students could see we were united, but also to show them how bad behaviors could really disrupt their learning. Eventually, JP was removed from the academy and sent to the Spanish-speaking SPED (Special Education) program. After three weeks there, it was decided that he was not SPED, just a serious pain. His sidekick, RM, became a different person and behaved. DJR was threatened with expulsion if he didn't change, after which he, very quickly, modified his own behavior. By the time JP came back to the academy, RM and DJR realized how they had started learning and pulled away from him. Ultimately, JP's father couldn't handle his altercations and decided to send him back to the Dominican Republic. For the three years that I taught at NBPMS until I excessed myself out (placed my name in a pool of teachers who were looking to be assigned elsewhere), I grew to love my students and to earn their trust. I also learned how much they didn't know anything about Haiti, and how nationalistic they could be. The Puerto Ricans' as well as the Dominicans' nationalisms also somewhat hindered their desire to learn the gringos' language. After all, Puerto Rico, although a commonwealth of the United States, is still a sort of colony, and the people are resisting through various forms of cultural maintenance.

OVERALL VIEW ON TEACHING

Serving a monolingual and non-diverse group of American students would already be a challenge for a teacher hoping to effectively educate while expanding the worldview of his or her students. In the culturally and linguistically diverse classroom, the prospect of successful teaching may be even more elusive.

Regardless of the composition of the students in front of you, understand that each student has a unique set of attributes, and every year—occurrences within your students' confined communities and daily lives will have a significant impact on what they bring to the classroom. Each of your students will be different, and your teaching must draw from those differences, meaning your curriculum and methods of instruction must be constantly reconsidered, revised, and renewed.

So, if teaching a non-diverse monolingual population is challenging, then teaching a diverse monolingual group would be even more challenging due to the array of needs, proficiencies, and competing subcultural narratives such a group will inevitably bring. And once you add a diverse and multilingual population of English learners to the mix, the challenge becomes even greater. Your classroom is now a United Nations of sociocultural, linguistic, and academic needs. Once again, regardless of the classroom's composition, what is clear is that a good, creative, and curious teacher will always treat his or her students as individuals with specific needs, and the students' particularities will remain at the forefront because the teacher is willing to engage the students in a culturally relevant way without forcing assimilation. Forced assimilation or acculturation will likely produce resistance, especially if there has been a negative relational history between the United States and the student's home country.

If a teacher is already curious, respectful, fair, knowledgeable, and passionate about the profession of teaching, then the mission to seriously educate students in communicating the required knowledge and skill sets is already grounded in a strong foundation; now, the challenge is transferring a human connection through the classroom-related activities of knowledge-making and problem-solving. Regardless of the constitution of the student body within a school or a classroom, as long as the gap of literacy or knowledge production is not major, an effective educator will expose his or her students to two fundamental aspects of teaching and learning, which are: (1) being a broadcaster of knowledge and (2) being a facilitator of knowledge. As such, through his or her democratic, comprehensive, and infectious ways of teaching, the effective teacher becomes a catalyst in the lives of each pupil as they prepare for an array of socio-professional roles. I am reminded of Robert L. Fried who, in his book *The Passionate Teacher*, writes:

> Passionate teachers have the capacity for spontaneity and humor and for great seriousness, often at almost the same time. They join with kids in appreciating the abundant absurdity of human nature but are also sensitive to issues that deserve to be taken seriously, particularly fairness and decency in how people treat one another. They try to build a culture of mutual respect amid societal pressures to stigmatize and condemn unpopular persons and ideas and to dismiss young people and their concerns.[15]

We have to constantly remind ourselves that young people are future adults, and therefore might be our future bosses, colleagues, caretakers, representatives, law enforcers, and even criminals. A professional civil servant who embodies knowledge is inherently a skill-builder for the future generations. The moment you step into the classroom as a professional adult, your personal prejudices, dilemmas, and strifes must remain outside or sealed away so that you will not pollute the learning environment.

Additionally, an effective teacher must essentially be a reflective teacher. Your life's geography must be a constant road of how you interact with others, and negative or the booby-trapped roads must always be avoided as you are guiding your students toward their own futures. Hence, if you have encountered difficulties or challenges in your own life, instead of becoming bitter and vengeful, you must be constantly striving toward becoming a better person. A complete human being whose purpose is to showcase what's beautiful about humanity without being naïve. Therefore, having that ability to empathize or sympathize, you intrinsically know that your students, diverse or not, are complex psychological beings who are embedded with their own histories. Ostensibly, an effective teacher knows that each child's personal geography has social, economic, political, historical, and psychological portals or checkpoints that must be taken into consideration when interacting with them. The classroom is not just a site that has chairs, books, blackboards, teachers, and students. A classroom is an integrated site of knowledge that has societal issues operating within it. Hence, most educators know (and *all* should) that when an educator incorporates an appreciative and empathic quality into their teaching style or teaching philosophy, this foundation of trust and nurturing of relationships creates a solid platform for effective teaching and relating to students.

TOWARD THE FUTURE

If the educational trends in both Haiti and the Dominican Republic can predict or indicate broader changes, then the pursuit of responsible citizenship must cease to be just a national endeavor to form individuals to serve industry needs and bureaucratic policies. These aspects by no means vanish; however, quality civic education and global competencies would forcibly push schools away from a nationalistically homogeneous education toward a multipronged education where the knowledge assets of civic education and globally oriented citizenship become more focused on empowering individuals who are not limited by national citizenship. Expressed differently, poverty, exploitation, and dysfunction shouldn't be what rights-oriented nations aspire to.

Haiti and the Dominican Republic certainly have different histories with regard to human rights violations, and both need to mend their own internal dilemmas and contradictions. However, the core of citizenship reform through progressive education must be a curriculum that places the discourse of human rights and sustainable development at its center. Likewise, there must be an emphasis on curriculum that vows to champion women's rights, justice, the environment, democracy, and freedom. As former colonies, and hyper-exploited societies, we must look to countries like Singapore that moved from Third World to First World by pushing an aggressive educational agenda. Our teachers must also be global citizens without jeopardizing their national identities. The fabric of their pedagogical philosophies must be embedded with broader global visions of development and a borderless mindset of post-national citizenship where collaborations to tackle pressing issues are always at the forefront.

Both Haiti and the Dominican Republic need to adopt global citizenship education in order to mitigate future conflict and evolve as resourceful partners in managing this tropical island that is in danger of collapse due to a lack of green development and an over-dependency on cash crops that were prevalent during the colonial period. Haiti and the Dominican Republic must also tackle green technology and sustainable development projects such hydroponic gardens and organic fisheries in order to alleviate pressures on and from the environment. Hence, science, technology, and mathematics (STEM) must play pivotal roles in the development of the future generation if we want to move away from the exotic realm into the productive and planet-centered realm. Quality education would certainly translate into productive and creative citizenship and therefore boost our overall Human Development Index. One would hope that both societies would seek to encapsulate the authority of truth in order to materialize the totality of their citizenries' human potential, which has never been realized given the structural colonial experiences and the remnants of institutional dictatorships.

With the large number of professional Haitians and Dominicans living abroad, it is absolutely possible to retool the two countries if each country's leadership has the willingness to make education a tool for human capital development, economic growth and moral achievements as well.

Chapter 2

TELL ALL THE OTHERS OUR STORY

Marie Lily Cerat

I know some people who just don't want to say that they're Haitians because it is associated with bad things. I think like learning about all these [Haitian linguistic and cultural practices], will give people this confidence in saying I am Haitian. That's who I am.

NINTH-GRADER GERALDINE, 2016

Exclusion has no place in twenty-first-century America. Yet the voices of Haitian youth in the New York City public school system convey otherwise. Comments from youngsters such as the high schooler Geraldine, quoted above, reflect various issues confronting these children. Accounts of the Haitian students highlighted in this document were collected from a series of focus groups and ethnographic interviews conducted in 2016 as part of a research project on Haitian linguistic and

---

In December 2016, I conducted a series of focus groups and ethnographic interviews with ten Haitian adolescents attending the New York City public schools. The sessions were on Haitian linguistic and cultural practices, and held on the site of Flanbwayan Haitian Literacy Project, a Brooklyn-based organization that works with Haitian newcomers in high school. To protect the confidentiality and privacy of the youth, their names have been changed.

cutural practices. The project was designed to assess whether Haitian practices such as *rara* and *vèvè*, among others, held any meanings for Haitian children living in the US.[1] The participants were youth members of Flanbwayan Haitian Literacy Project, a Brooklyn-based organization that works with Haitian newcomers attending high school.

THUS SPOKE THE CHILDREN

Close examination of the language used by the youngsters to speak of Haitian linguistic and cultural practices along with their schooling experiences in the New York City public schools illustrates both identity crisis[2] and academic disengagement due to curricula that do not include or validate their Haitian experience.[3] The language is symptomatic of their fears, apprehensions, and hopes. To ignore them is to fail "to recognize what is happening and think very seriously about the alarming consequences for all of us if we do nothing,"[4] as educational researcher Gary Orfield and coauthors caution in a 2012 report on the dire state of segregation in US schools.[5] To put it differently, the words of these Haitian children matter.

In addition to the long open secret that the nation's school systems—including New York's—are still struggling with desegregation, the achievement gap for minority students remains equally persistent. Performance assessment data on English Language Learners (ELLs) in the New York City public school system—the largest in the nation—which comprises a large swath of Haitian Creole–speaking students, are extremely concerning. While ELL performance data are not disaggregated for specific languages, no language community can celebrate these numbers. For academic years 2018 and 2019, only 9 percent of ELLs from grades three to eight tested proficient on the English Language Arts exam. In math, 16 percent were proficient in 2018 and 17 percent in 2019. The high school graduation rate for ELLs rose slightly in 2019 to 41 percent compared to 34.7 percent the previous year. By all accounts, these are dismal numbers. They reflect the structural issues in the system.

By shedding light on the words of the Haitian youngsters, we hope to gain understanding of the various factors that have influenced and formed the context in which they find it difficult to affirm their Haitian identity, and to identify what can help them develop, "this confidence in saying, 'I am Haitian. That's who I am,'" as Geraldine states. Specifically, their language may: open a window to understanding what creates the conditions in which they "just don't want to say that they're Haitians," provide insights about their teaching and learning experiences inside the New York City public school system, and suggest interventions that can improve their educational outcomes and better prepare them to become proud and contributing citizens in the society.

AS MORE PEOPLE DREAM
A Brief History of Haiti and Haitian Immigration to the United States from 1956 to 2016

To grasp the meaning and potency of the language used by the Haitian youngsters to describe their experiences in the New York City public school system, an overview of the history of Haiti and Haitian immigration to the United States from approximately 1956 to 2016 proves indispensable, for the source of these youngsters' language or words is informed by historical experiences from both contexts.[6]

Unquestionably, sociopolitical tempests in Haiti between approximately 1956 and 2016 tossed a great number of Haitians—young and old—to the shores of its most prosperous neighbor. Nearly half a million people left Haiti to migrate to the United States, settling primarily in cities like Boston, Chicago, Miami, and New York.[7] Numerous scholars contend that the catalyst for most of the people who left Haiti in the late 1950s and throughout the 1960s was the ascendance to power of François (Papa Doc) Duvalier in 1957.[8]

Without a doubt, that first major wave can be attributed to various internal factors created by Duvalier and buttressed by external forces. Along with the rise of the repressive Duvalier dictatorship, which limited nearly all liberties (i.e., freedom of speech, freedom of the press, right to assemble, etc.),[9] came the further spiraling-down of Haiti's economy,[10] accompanied by internal corruption such as misappropriation of state revenues, plundering of international aids and loans, and the "head in the sand" attitude of the international community on human rights abuses in the country.[11] Combined, these factors indeed contributed to the flight of countless intellectuals, trained professionals, young and old, whoever could afford a way out.[12]

When the younger despot Jean Claude (Baby Doc) Duvalier replaced his father after his death in 1971, the external migration or flight from the homeland toward other shores and skies multiplied.[13] The surge from 1970 to the mid-1980s saw a lot of people desperately seeking any and all means to leave the *unlivable* Haiti. Records from the US Office of Immigration Statistics show that about 175,000 Haitians obtained lawful permanent residency in the United States alone.[14] Besides applying for all types of foreign visas (i.e., student, visitor, seasonal worker, contract laborer, etc.) for various countries, thousands more would chance it on the open sea in poorly constructed and overcrowded boats in the hopes of reaching the Florida coast or some other Caribbean islands along the way, where they believed they would fare better than in Haiti. The desperation observed with many in this wave of migration brings to mind the title of the 2003 debut album of the African American rapper 50 Cent: *Get Rich or Die Tryin'*. Any story on the Haitian "fleet" of unseaworthy vessels on the treacherous

Windward Passage and North Atlantic Ocean could have been titled: *Leave Alive or Die Trying*. Many did survive. But several boats capsized, and countless died during the perilous journey.

Haitians who fled Baby Doc's 1980s Haiti aboard a *kanntè* —the name for the makeshift vessels on which they sailed— and reached the Florida shore or were intercepted by the US Coast Guard were thrown into US detention centers on the continental United States and its outposts like Puerto Rico.[15] Labeled "economic migrants" rather than political refugees like the Cubans,[16] the US government would drag its feet on the fate of the Haitians as they waited in detention for US courts and immigration policymakers and implementers to explore how to handle their cases: whether they would be admitted as political asylum seekers or be repatriated to Haiti.[17]

Of the facilities used to incarcerate the Haitians in the 1980s, the Krome Detention Center in Florida would receive the most visibility. The involvement of US leaders, such as the African American Reverend Jesse Jackson, decrying the racist and inhumane treatment of the Haitian detainees at Krome, including pressures from Haitian community leaders and human rights advocates, drew enormous attention to their plight. Conscious of their conditions, the detainees themselves did not remain entirely apathetic. Michel Laguerre notes: "During the Christmas season of 1981, the detainees at Krome staged a hunger strike . . . [while] sympathetic demonstrators, including representatives of the NAACP and the Union of American Hebrew Congregations" demonstrated outside to denounce their unfair treatment.[18] Such public actions brought greater light to the incarceration of Haitians who were escaping the brutal dictatorship of Baby Doc. Out of that era, the Krome Center came to symbolize the unjust and racist treatment of Haitians seeking safe haven at the hands of the United States.

It was also in that same period monikers like "Haitian boat

people" and "Haitian refugees" were born. The two terms were used by US immigration policymakers and national and international media, as well as by advocates to discuss the situation of the Haitian detainees. However, the two expressions would later acquire derogatory connotations, and they became used as insults against Haitian immigrants.

They think that just because we are Black, we're inferior and they're superior. I can say that we're not inferior. Just because our pigmentation is different from them doesn't mean we are different from them. Because we work hard as much as them: to feed our families, to have a better life, [and] to go to school. Sometimes people are mistreating us and don't know how it feels. But we still keep going because we know we have to do better. But it hurts a lot when they discriminate against you because of the color of your skin. The way they treat you different as if you are not a human being.

ELEVENTH-GRADER MIREILLE, 2016

Deteriorating conditions in Haiti following the departure of Jean Claude (Baby Doc) Duvalier in 1986, along with the situation of the detainees in US centers like Krome greatly preoccupied Haitian immigrants in the United States.[19] Yet US Haitian immigrants also face additional local challenges. The 1988 release of the horror movie *The Serpent and the Rainbow*, loosely based on the research of the American ethnobotanist Wade Davis on the *zonbi* phenomenon in Haiti, transformed Vodou, the African-based belief system of Haitians, into a culture of zombie-making.[20] Already misunderstood, people completely unfamiliar with the Haitian cultural tradition would equate the practice to devil worship and black magic. Vodou *lwa* (spirits) were characterized as bad and maleficent. As a result, Haitian

Vodou and its practitioners would be further demonized, and ridiculed.

Then came the tumultuous 1990s. Following the bloody coup d'état in September 1991 against the popular priest-turned-president Jean-Bertrand Aristide, nearly the same migratory escape routes and scenes of the 1980s were replayed.[21] While Aristide was whisked off into exile, some of the urban poor and peasants that elected him were being tortured and killed by the putschist Haitian military and other anti-Aristide factions. This prompted many of his supporters to begin fleeing for their lives aboard fishing boats or anything that could float.

Six months after the overthrow of Aristide, more than fifteen thousand Haitians were intercepted at sea by the US Coast Guard and encamped at the US naval base on Guantánamo Bay in Cuba.[22] Like Krome in the 1980s, Guantánamo is etched in Haitian memory as the 1990s US concentration camp for the thousands of Haitians seeking refuge from the political violence that engulfed Haiti. The historical layers of the Guantánamo US Naval Base also include the court battle between the US government and Yale Law students and professor Harold Koh—on behalf of the 1990s' Haitian detainees, including some 120 who had tested positive for HIV.[23] Koh and his students challenged the US government in court on the detainment of the Haitians, as well as the legality and constitutionality of denying political asylum to individuals with "well-founded fear of persecution" on the basis of their illnesses, and won.[24]

Early into the twenty-first century, catastrophe upon catastrophe descended on Haiti.[25] On January 12, 2010, only eleven days after Haitians celebrated the 206th anniversary of their anti-slavery revolution and 1804 independence, the devastating 7.0 magnitude earthquake hit the feeble nation.[26] More than a quarter-million people died in the earthquake, and millions instantly became homeless.[27] In the blink of an eye that

January afternoon, Haiti's capital city of Port-au-Prince lay in ruins, becoming a mass grave for thousands of its inhabitants.[28] Léogâne, a western town situated some sixteen miles from Port-au-Prince, was the epicenter of the earthquake. It suffered a massive loss of human lives and home damage as significant as in the capital city. However, media attention overcrowded the densely populated Port-au-Prince, which also housed all government offices, eclipsing coverage of the destruction of the smaller town.

Six years later, in October 2016, Hurricane Matthew served another devastating blow to the poorly prepared Haiti, already suffering from little to no infrastructure. The Category 4 hurricane would cause some eight hundred deaths and the displacement and homelessness of thousands more.[29]

The consistent man-made and natural disasters in those six decades—1956 to 2016—further incapacitated and impoverished Haiti.[30] Clearly, these human and environmental tragedies hugely contributed to making Haiti the difficult place it has been for Haitians, forcing *many*—young and old—to leave the country for other lands like the United States where the possibility of living a safe and dignified life seems attainable.

The undated popular folkloric Haitian *rara* song below suddenly acquires deeper meanings. It captures the reality for Haitians in a collective voice, and amplifies the people's endless cry as they search for a better life:

> M rele woy lamizè pa dous o
> Anmwe yyy wo
> (Mezanmi lamizè pa dous tande)
> M rele woy lamizè pa dous o
> Anmwe yyy wo
> M rele woy lamizè pa dous o
> Anmwe yyy wo, m pral chache lavi a on lòt kote woy!

[I am screaming that misery is not sweet
Help
(My friends, misery is not sweet)
I am screaming that misery is not sweet
Help
I am screaming that misery is not sweet
Help, I am going to look for life someplace else]

This cry for help and search for life in other lands—particularly in the United States—does not mean that Haitians are ever welcome with open arms. In effect, Haitian immigrants in the United States are frequently subjected to racist narratives, policies, and actions, both officially and unofficially, giving credence to Geraldine's words that being Haitian "is associated with bad things."

One recent public illustration occurred in December of 2017, when it was widely reported in the US media that President Donald J. Trump used derogatory terms to speak of Haiti and its immigrants at a White House meeting with policymakers.[31] Well known for his vulgarity, the forty-fifth president is alleged to have referred to Haiti as one of the nations he considers to be "shithole countries," and to have said: "All Haitians have AIDS." That a couple of officials present felt obliged to expose the president indicates their uneasiness, in addition to how racist and vile his comments were. Let's note here that US officials making racist statements about Haiti and Haitians did not begin with Mr. Trump. The forty-fifth president is only the latest.[32]

THE TRAGEDY OF HAITIAN YOUTH GOING UNDERCOVER

In the 1990s, many Haitian youngsters in the New York area referred to some of their Haitian peers as HU, an abbreviation that meant *Haitian Undercover*.[33] What circulated was these youth kept their Haitian ethnic identity *undercover* to prevent ostracization from non-Haitian peers. This moniker surfaced on the heels of the 1990 announcement by the Food and Drug Administration (FDA), the US institution charged with safe-guarding the nation's blood supply, of a policy that banned Haitians from donating blood because they were identified as a carrier group for HIV and AIDS.[34]

The FDA policy broadcast felt as earth-shattering for Hai-tians around the world as the 2010 earthquake in Haiti would be received twenty years later. There was shock, confusion, and embarrassment. In the days that followed the FDA's public statement, US Haitian immigrants held endless community meetings and had heated debates on the scientific soundness of the policy. But ultimately, every Haitian recognized the *racism* behind the policy.

On April 20, 1990, Haitian immigrants in New York from all walks of life held one of the largest public demonstrations in the country to call out the racist policy of the FDA and the Centers for Disease Control and Prevention (CDC), the nation's leading health institution, which had previously classified Haitians as a high-risk group for AIDS.[35] While pressures from the Haitian community and their allies forced these institutions to rescind the policy, the hurt to Haitian pride could not be undone. The re-peal of the publicly announced policy by the FDA and the CDC would be too little to repair the damage. In the end, the HIV/AIDS ordeal left all Haitians feeling indignant, humiliated, and ashamed, and it became a catalyst for some Haitian youth in New York to begin to hide their Haitian identity in the 1990s.

In *Storming the Court*, Brandt Goldstein explains why the 1992 court filing by Yale Law students and professor Harold Koh on behalf of the Haitian detainees on Guantánamo, in-cluding some 120 diagnosed with HIV/AIDS, initially omitted the HIV cases.[36] He writes:

Haitian boat people were hardly a popular group. Haitians with AIDS would be the most unsympathetic plaintiffs imaginable. The stereotypes and fear surrounding HIV remained extreme at the time. . . . Haitians in America faced particularly harsh prejudice relating to HIV. Years earlier, the federal Centers for Disease Control and Prevention had branded them as a high-risk group for the disease. . . . [Haitians] found themselves under especially vicious attack. Some watched their businesses fail; others were evicted from their apartments; Haitian children were beaten in school. Graffiti in Brooklyn proclaimed: "Haitians = Niggers with AIDS." Challenging the HIV rule before a judge . . . was risky.[37]

The strategy of staying *undercover* by Haitian youngsters in New York was not a new phenomenon. Both young and old Haitians have, at times, had to hide their identity to escape discrimination.

Alex Stepick's 1998 book *Pride Against Prejudice: Haitians in the United States* documents the poignant story of a young Haitian man in Miami named Phede Eugene, who committed suicide.[38] Stepick relates that the Haitian immigrant high schooler went to great lengths to "cover up" his Haitian identity. Phede refused to speak Haitian Creole, the native language of all or most Haitians in public, "Americanizing his name" to Fred to avoid the stigmatization and discrimination hanging over the heads of Haitians in Miami, and in places like New York City.[39] A good student, a member of his church chorale, Phede— known by his peers as Fred—also had a job. However, Phede or Fred became so distraught when his sister spoke Haitian Creole with him in front of his African American girlfriend, thereby "outing" him as Haitian, that a few days later "he bought a .22 caliber revolver for $50, drove to an empty lot near his home, and killed himself with a bullet to his chest."[40]

AND THE SAGA PLAYED ON

The years following the HIV/AIDS 1990 policy debacle by the CDC and FDA showed a more significant number of Haitian youngsters in New York pretending to belong to other nationalities and hiding their Haitian identity for their "social survival."[41] This rise in the 1990s of New York Haitian youngsters in college and high school concealing or disguising their identities was clearly a means to cope with vicious attacks directed at the community in the midst of the HIV/AIDS pandemonium.[42] Here, Haitians, one ethnic group, were singled out and publicly labeled as carriers of one of the world's most fatal and stigmatized diseases. Research on HIV was still mostly in its early stages, and the disease was not yet fully understood. Everyone was afraid.[43] Many people became particularly afraid of Haitians, worried that any casual contact with Haitians could give them HIV/AIDS. The whole experience made it an awfully difficult time for all Haitians—inside and outside of Haiti—and particularly for the youth.

The research on adolescents and young adults indicates that it is between the ages of fourteen and nineteen that a sense of self is developed.[44] As a result, adolescents and young adults frequently struggle with issues of identity, can become increasingly influenced by peers, and perceive social connections such as making friends and being popular as important. How else could Haitian youth handle or cope with being perceived by their peers as a carrier of the deadly AIDS virus? While problematic and alarming—recall the case of Phede—the approach taken by these New York Haitian youngsters can be framed as a survival strategy[45] or "social survival."[46]

To conceal their Haitian ethnic identity, some New York youth refused to speak Haitian Creole in public, changed their speech patterns, changed their names, and appropriated other mannerisms, all to try to pass as other than Haitian.[47] Recall ninth-grader Geraldine, who observed, "I know some people who just don't want to say that they're Haitians because it is associated with bad things." That said, the Haitian youth that engage in this identity concealing or identity disguising practice use the tactics to disassociate themselves from the "bad things" associated with being Haitian.[48]

Let's note that the phenomenon of identity concealing or identity disguising is not unique to Haitians. Groups that are "othered" or considered as "other" in certain contexts have, at times, needed to hide their identities to deflect prejudices and biases. For example, many in the German American community altered or anglicized the spelling of their surnames, among other strategies, to *cover* their ethnic identity as anti-German sentiment and xenophobia increased during the two world wars.[49] It helped to cope with the situation, as well as to blend in with the larger white population.

The strategy employed by Haitian youth has been used to escape alienating, shaming, racist, and xenophobic policies such as the state-sanctioned HIV/AIDS 1990 policy by the CDC and the FDA and public narratives like the street graffiti in Brooklyn that read "Haitians = Niggers with AIDS," coming from the larger community.[50] This stratagem was also used to blend in with the larger Black population and evade the Haitian AIDS stigma.[51]

It is clear that even today, the false assertion that all Haitians are carriers of AIDS persists, and seemingly weighs on policy decisions regarding Haitian immigrants to the US when one considers President Trump's remarks at that cabinet meeting.[52] His utterances exemplified the high-level sources for some of the discriminatory narratives and racist policy practices that Haitian immigrants can be subjected to at times in this country, and which cause some Haitian young adults to feel that they must disguise or hide their Haitianness or "just don't want to say that they're Haitians because it is associated with bad things" as Geraldine underscores. While hiding their Haitian identity can be viewed as a survival strategy, it has serious implications. Phede's case provides a sobering illustration about the worst possible outcome. We must consider the potential psychoemotional and social issues and fears with which some Haitian young adults must live lest their ethnic identity be revealed or uncovered. What must schools be doing to help these young people develop a healthy sense of self and become well-adjusted citizens?

HAITIAN YOUTH IN NEW YORK CITY PUBLIC SCHOOLS
SPEAKING UP AND SPEAKING OUT

In his 2001 book *Negotiating Identities: Education for Empowerment in a Diverse Society*, the educational scholar Jim Cummins pointedly remarks:

> Schools reflect the values and attitudes of the broader society that supports them and so it is hardly surprising that in the United States students from African American, Latino/Latina, and Native American communities have experienced extensive devaluation of their cultures and languages [and histories] within the school context. In some cases, students perceive their identity is endangered by this process of devaluation and consequently drop out of school in order to preserve their sense of self.[53]

Students of Haitian ancestry that enter the New York City public schools are already burdened by enduring stereotypes propagated throughout the society—like boat people, HIV/ AIDS carrier, Vodou practitioner, or zombie-making people, and so on—that force them to engage in the identity conceal- ing or identity disguising strategy. Yet they also expressed facing other challenges in schools that can further "endanger" their identity or damage their sense of self. That is, the exclusion or absence of educational programs in schools that validate Hai- tian Creole language and culture introduces an additional layer of complexity.

> *Some Haitians don't want to speak [Haitian] Creole at school. I know the value at home. I tried to speak [Hai- tian] Creole with a friend. He said speak English. I asked why? He said because we're in public. I was like. I was so confused. I am like, what about the other kids that speak their language? He was . . . I was . . . Why can't we speak our language? Then he was looking like he was embar- rassed. Then I leave it alone, cause—yeah . . .*
>
> NINTH-GRADER GERALDINE, 2016

That Haitian students in the New York City public schools feel "embarrassed" to speak their Haitian Creole language in school in the year 2016, as Geraldine recounts, points to the con- tinuing endangerment to these children's identity, and exposes the failure of the schools to support them. Moreover, this iden- tity crisis is connected to, and forms part of, the causes for the serious and ongoing educational crises observed with these chil- dren. That is, academic disengagement, poor quality work, ac- ademic underperformance, environmental alienation, dropout, and so on. In other words, the schooling experiences of Haitian children in the New York City public school system add to their sense of alienation in the society. This should alarm all of us.

*There's a certain way the society looks at you. I want to
change that. I want to know why they keep this part of my
culture away from us. Why do they keep it away? And the
things they're teaching you, teaching me. . . . They have
nothing related to my culture. They teach us about slavery.
Really? But they never teach us about the whole history of
slavery. And then it's like they're putting this thing into our
mind that, OK, slavery happened. But they expect us to
forget what happened. And I can't forget what happened.
Even though I did not participate. Even though I did not
suffer from it. But I still suffer now because I have been
affected by racism. People have been racist to me.*

TWELFTH-GRADER MONIQUE, 2016

One Haitian youth pointedly stated, "I don't even want to
be there." The youngsters described the school environment as
a place that made them feel embarrassed about who they are,
their practices, and having to hide their Haitian identity for
fear of alienation and stigmatization. This is a direct reflection
of what is occurring in the larger society when national media
outlets report that the President of the United States himself
engages in derogatory "Haitian name-calling."

In effect, Haitian youngsters are far from being alone, when
they can echo other prominent voices like the African American
writer and journalist Ta-Nehisi Coates (a former student of the
Baltimore public schools), who in his 2015 memoir *Between the
World and Me* offers a scathing critique about the ways in which
the Baltimore public school system treats and treated its Black
students. Coates writes: "If the streets shackled my right leg, the
schools shackled my left. . . . I suffered at the hands of both,
but I resent the schools more. . . . I sensed the schools were
hiding something, drugging us with false morality. . . . Schools
did not reveal truths, they concealed them."[54] Statements from

the Haitian students and Coates illustrate what children from oppressed communities continuously experience in the public schools. And institutions, like schools, unquestionably mirror society, as Jim Cummins cautions. But why do the public schools continue to be such alienating spaces for Black children in twenty-first-century America?

Schools should teach drums. Haitian drumming. In the time of slavery the slaves especially utilized the drums to have their own celebrations. When the masters gave them some free time, they would dance, though the masters mistreated them. Although they would be beaten while they worked, they'd beat the drums to express how they felt. Even though they were enduring great misery, even though the masters were beating them, they had no food, but they still felt grateful and thankful that they were still alive and they danced.

NINTH-GRADER CAROLINE, 2016

According to research conducted in 2012 and 2014 by the Civil Rights Project at the University of California, Los Angeles, schools in the United States have remained unchanged despite the historic 1954 *Brown v. Board of Education of Topeka* legal case, which annulled the doctrine of "separate but equal" and mandated the integration of the nation's schools. One of the UCLA Civil Rights Project reports published in 2014 to mark the sixtieth anniversary of *Brown* and which was intended to gauge and evaluate the impact of *Brown* on schools in the nation, claimed that: "New York has the most segregated schools" in the nation.[55] Negligent educational practices, as per researchers like Orfield and Kucsera and recounted by the Haitian youngsters, are occurring and persisting in our schools despite existing legal precedents like *Brown*.

In addition to *Brown*, there were myriad additional legal measures that followed to ensure that minority children—like the Haitian students—were receiving a quality education that would address their cultural and linguistic needs. The 1965 federal Elementary and Secondary Education Act (ESEA)—in its former and present iterations—the 1968 Bilingual Education Act (BEA), and the 1974 cases *Lau v. Nichols* and *Aspira v. Board of Education of New York* were all decided or enacted to remedy the poor educational conditions for Black and Brown children, to redress inequities, and to provide these children with an education that includes and responds to their academic needs using, or at least including, the language and culture they bring with them to schools. Had these laws and mandates—ratified to ensure the academic, linguistic, and cultural needs of minority children—not been ignored, Haitian students, and particularly those who enter the New York City public school system not yet having learned the English language, would not have to fear speaking their Haitian Creole language, both in and out of school.

On the contrary, Haitian children in the New York City public school system should have the opportunity to enter educational settings or bilingual education programs where they receive content area instruction in both their Haitian native language and English, Native Language Arts, and English as a Second Language as instructed by the US Supreme Court in the 1974 Lau consent decree, as well as in the Aspira consent decree in New York. These legal agreements were to further strengthen and support the 1954 *Brown* decision and the 1968 Bilingual Education Act, to ensure educational equity and to attend to the educational achievement of Black and Brown children in our schools.[56]

It is concerning for the New York City public school system, where the majority of its more than one million students hail from communities of color and 72.8 percent are economically disadvantaged and 13.2 percent are categorized as English Language Learners to only have *one* bilingual Haitian program at the high school level and *two* programs at the elementary and middle school levels to serve Haitian children.[57] How is the system meeting the needs of or appropriately serving the more than three thousand Haitian children identified as newcomers or students who require Bilingual Education services?

It is rather alarming that there are only *three* public schools in the New York City Department of Education with bilingual education programs for Haitian students. The absence of such programs—including bilingual Haitian Creole teachers, guidance counselors, psychologists, and so on—contributes to Haitian youngsters fearing speaking their native language on school grounds. The exclusion of the Haitian Creole language in the education of Haitian Creole–speaking students reinforces negative attitudes about the Creole language in society in general, and signals to these youngsters and the larger population that Haitian Creole has no value.

A 2019 research study conducted by Flanbwayan, which assists Haitian immigrant youth families to negotiate the bureaucracy of the New York City school system in enrolling their children, found there are no structures in place to

> provide [these] young people the information that they need to make choices about which schools to attend, . . . information that is crucial to their understanding of the New York City high school system or the types of schools and programs available to them. Without such information young people and their families cannot ask informed questions about their options, advocate for themselves, or make meaningful decisions.[58]

The dysfunctions of the system are such that the Flanbwayan report claimed to have found Haitian Creole–speaking students who had been "placed in a Spanish Bilingual program despite the fact that they do not speak Spanish."[59] Proper identification and placement of Haitian students, among other issues, has long been a problem with the system.[60] In the late 1990s, Haitian parents and advocates initiated a lawsuit alleging that the then New York City Board of Education (currently the New York City Department of Education) and the New York State Education Department of educational neglect of Haitian students, demanding that "the rights of Haitian national origin school children who speak Haitian Creole and have limited English proficiency to receive appropriate special education and bilingual services" to meet their academic, linguistic, and cultural needs.[61]

Such systemic malpractice, misplacement, and misidentification of Haitian students—and the lack of bilingual Haitian Creole programs to meet the academic, linguistic, and cultural needs of Haitian youngsters—violate their "linguistic human rights."[62] Rights that should be and must be afforded to *all* students regardless of race, creed, gender, sexual identification, language, and culture, among others, and that ought to be respected and upheld. Such rights ensure that *all* students, including Haitian youngsters, receive an education that validates and affirms their identities and enables them to be successful learners, living dignified lives, as they become productive members of society.

The school system's reluctance to serve multilingual and multicultural students is rooted in a calcified American racism borne out of the legacy of slavery and ensuing segregationist and separatist laws that followed the abolition of slavery in the nation. As such, the education of minority students, like the Haitians in the New York City public school system, remains under siege.

These ongoing and unfair practices, or malpractices, are occurring in twenty-first-century America, and despite warning by countless education scholars and advocates who have argued for years that the educational crises (i.e., academic underperformance, academic disengagement, poor quality academic work, dropout, etc.) observed with minority children are fueled by structural dysfunctions or systemic injustices built into the school system, and manifested through its failure or resistance to acknowledge and validate the language, culture, and history of Black children.[63]

In addition to the absence of programs in the language of Haitian youngsters, the students complained of finding versions and content of history as presented in school to be biased, and therefore, they *do not trust* the materials or their teachers.

I think it's important that they do [integrate Haitian linguistic and cultural practices in instructional activities]. Cause they tend to leave things out. Like recently, my dad was telling me about that, how slavery ended in Haiti, and that there were Haitian soldiers that helped America when they were trying to become free. And I never knew that. Cause they never say that in history books. So I was surprised. So they are leaving things out that they shouldn't. Because that's important in a way.

ELEVENTH-GRADER MIREILLE, 2016

All they tell us is that we were slaves and Abraham Lincoln liberated the slaves. That's not the whole story. It makes me think that what they are teaching in school is not the whole story. There is a different side to the story. I would change the way history is taught.

TWELFTH-GRADER MONIQUE, 2016

The Haitian youth repeatedly returned to the idea that something is missing in their schooling experience. They connect the absence of their language, culture, and history in instructional events to the presence of curricula that are biased and Eurocentric, and that do not provide "the whole story," or only provide one side of the story.

In his memoir or cautionary tale to his son about being Black in America, Ta-Nehisi Coates makes a comparable argument on the curriculum offered to him as a young Black student in the Baltimore public schools:

> The world had no time for black boys and girls. How could the schools? Algebra, Biology, and English were not subjects so much as opportunities to better discipline the body, to practice writing between the lines, copying directions legibly, memorizing theorems extracted from the world they were created to represent. All of it felt distant to me. . . . I was a curious boy, but the schools were not concerned with curiosity. . . . I loved a few of my teachers. But I cannot say that I truly believed any of them.[64]

Similarly, the Haitian youth expressed that the exclusion of their history, language, and culture as part of their schooling or instructional experiences erodes their confidence and pride in their identities as students of color. The youngsters voiced that the system engages in practices that undermine their ways of knowing and doing—their historical experiences—which, thereby, discourages academic engagement and limits their achievement.

> *I don't really like school. They don't teach you anything.*
> *I don't even want to be there.*
>
> TENTH-GRADER CARLO, 2016

In their own words, the Haitian youth speaking up and speaking out throughout this document join scholars like Lisa Delpit, Gloria Ladson-Billings and William Tate, and Shawn A. Ginwright, among others, who have long been calling for a pedagogy that makes relevant the culture, language, and history of Black children. Ginwright offers a compelling argument about what schools can do to educate, nurture, and engage minority students like the Haitians. He contends:

> African culture and philosophy is simply too valuable to discount. . . . [W]e should continue to challenge, push and develop African-centered scholarship and practice in ways that allow us to confront this crisis of black youth today. An emancipatory vision for black youth means that being rooted in African culture is a starting point for identity development, but not the end point. Our understanding of culture and identity development must be viewed as a pathway to justice and freedom. First, this requires an acknowledgment that African cultural identity is perhaps the most effective weapon to fight white supremacy. For black youth who internalize negative images of black people without knowing why, culture is a powerful vehicle to uncover their hidden shame of being black.[65]

Thus understood, it clearly does not suffice for schools, teachers, and textbooks to simply present students with one version of history, which leads the Haitian youngster Monique to eloquently say, "All they tell us is that we were slaves and Abraham Lincoln liberated the slaves. That's not the whole story." By not teaching all the versions and sides of history, schools robbed Black students and *all* students of accurate historical knowledge.[66] School systems, leaders, and teachers have a responsibility to create educational settings that can help minority children liberate themselves of the "shame of being Black," and thereby encourage Haitian students to affirm rather than to conceal and disguise their Haitian ethnic identity.[67]

In *Other People's Children: Cultural Conflict in the Classroom* (1995), Lisa Delpit argues:

> If we plan to survive as a species on this planet we must certainly create multicultural curricula that educate our children to the different perspectives of our diverse population. In part, the problems we see exhibited in school by African-American children and children of other oppressed minorities can be traced to this lack of a curriculum in which they can find represented the intellectual achievements of people who look like themselves. . . . Our children of color need to see the brilliance of their legacy, too.[68]

The Haitian youngsters' voices highlighted in this essay made comments that are consistent with the views of educational scholars like Delpit, Ginwright, and others about missed opportunities by schools to engage *all* children with a multicultural curriculum. The Haitian children thirst for curricula that offer and include perspectives and experiences beyond a Western, Eurocentric epistemology. In excluding Haitian epistemology and Haitian language, culture, and history, schools fail to help these children build on their ways of knowing and experiences and develop pride in their Haitian identity or as descendants of Africans.

In addition to learning about the emancipation of the American slaves in 1863 by President Abraham Lincoln, Black children should learn versions of history that illustrate the resistance of their African ancestors to the brutal and inhumane system of slavery, as many of the Haitian youth point out. For instance, American slaves like Denmark Vesey and Nat Turner who resisted the system and sought opportunities to liberate their fellow slaves ought to be featured as heroes in American history, not simply appear as footnotes in texts. The history of slavery and slave resistance in America must also be part of the larger American story, part of the American democratic project that involves *all* citizens.

History lessons could cover the anti-slavery Haitian Revolution, followed by independence in 1804, when African slaves and their descendants on colonial French Saint-Domingue (present-day Haiti) overturned the system of slavery. This victory for human rights achieved by the slaves over their masters represents a significant milestone in the transatlantic history of slavery in the New World. It embodies humanistic ideals such as the equality of all and "the unalienable rights" to "life, liberty and the pursuit of happiness" that are foundational to American democracy. The Haitian accomplishment inspired many oppressed communities throughout the Western Hemisphere to advocate for freedom, from the South American liberator Simón Bolívar to the Black American abolitionist Frederick Douglass.[69]

Exposure to the Haitian slaves' historical triumph over human bondage, coupled with core values like democracy and equality at the foundation of America can serve to deepen students' understanding of human rights. All learners can draw inspiration from the visions and accomplishments of great Americans like Abraham Lincoln, Harriet Tubman, Frederick Douglass, or the Haitian liberator Jean-Jacques Dessalines. All these leaders believed in the common humanity of *all*—children, women, and men—and the rights of all people to live free and in a world where they are respected and protected.

In 2018, New York State Assemblywoman Rodneyse Bichotte, an American of Haitian descent, spearheaded the initiative to name part of Rogers Avenue in Brooklyn as Jean-Jacques

Dessalines Boulevard to honor the Haitian founding father that envisioned a world without slavery.[70] Bichotte's endeavor was likely rooted in stories heard about the freedom fighter from her Haitian immigrant parents or during her schooling days at P.S. 189K—The Bilingual Center, where students are exposed to Haitian language, culture, and history through the bilingual program created to serve Haitian children and their families. Moreover, to realize the street naming project, Bichotte brought together various factions of the New York Haitian community along with their allies, thereby exemplifying the power of collective work and, the power of unity, some of the values that guided the Haitian liberator in that fight for freedom. Jean-Jacques Dessalines Boulevard runs through the heart of the Haitian community in the borough of Brooklyn. It helps validate the history and presence of the New York Haitian immigrant community, as well as acknowledges the community's contributions to the development of New York City.[71]

When school systems from New York City and around the nation embrace diversity and inclusion as cornerstones of the educational experience, they will teach Black, Brown, and white children "the whole story," as twelfth-grader Monique hopes, by including the history of enslaved Africans in Saint-Domingue who liberated themselves and created Haiti, the first Black and independent nation. Specifically, they will empower Black and Brown children, and in fact, really offer these children a transformative education. It will be an education that will equip these learners with the critical and creative thinking tools to take actions to change their condition, community, and society for the better.

Haitian independence in 1804 was, and remains, one of the most compelling counter-arguments to the false narrative of African inferiority used to justify the enslavement of more than eleven million Africans from the fifteenth to the nineteenth century in the New World.[72] Teaching about the transatlantic slave trade history as well as the success of the Haitian slaves' revolution to minority students changes the perception of slaves as passive victims to slaves as change agents. What child, if taught critical analysis skills, would not or cannot appreciate the significance and magnitude of this momentous history of humanity realized by the Haitian slaves? What Black child will not be inspired or gain a sense of pride in learning about the accomplishment of these African ancestors in the New World?

The Haitian youth envision school environments where their history, language, and culture would serve as foundational elements and building blocks to their learning. They yearn for school programming that includes Haitian musical traditions and instruments, Haitian proverbs, folktales, and modern literature, Haitian *vèvè* diagrams, cultural items that help them to develop the confidence to say: "I am Haitian. That's who I am."

When I have a problem to solve, I always think of a weird and crazy way to do it, to solve it. All of them [vèvè diagrams] would be useful. This one would be very great with graphs. Like math for example, teaching someone how to label plot, create a heart, label plot. They can give you two coordinates and just tell you to plot it down and find it. This one really actually looks like a graph line! And you can actually use it to figure out the coordinates of these small shapes, axes. They are very complicated stuff.

NINTH-GRADER CAROLINE, 2016

Caroline, cited above, and some other youngsters comment on how useful *vèvè* diagrams would be in teaching mathematics. Linda, quoted below, shares that her knowledge and use of Haitian proverbs with her family contributed to the development of her English writing skills. Her experience serves to exemplify what schools and programs that incorporate and include Haitian cultural practices could accomplish for Haitian learners. Bilingual educators have long understood that students are capable of transferring skills learned from one language to another.

The African-based cultural traditions found in Haitian practices were recreated in the context of slavery. Drum rhythms and dances, memories and souvenirs of African philosophy (i.e., proverbs, stories, ways of relating to the universe and one another, ways of being and knowing, etc.) from the minds of the captives/enslaved became significant elements for the reconstruction of their being/existence, and ultimately became tools for resistance and survival. For Haitian youngsters and all Black children, these practices matter. They matter for their academic, social, and emotional adjustment and success.

> *My parents use a lot of [Haitian Creole] proverbs. The language itself is so great and different. The use of metaphors is extremely there. I remember when my mom came she was forcing me to eat vegetables. And I don't want to eat, and she was "ou ka fòse bourik janbe rivyè, men ou pa ka fòse l bwè dlo" [You can force a donkey to cross the river, but you cannot force it to drink water]. It [Haitian Creole] shapes like the use of figurative terms. That is why it was easier for me to learn to use figurative terms in my writing, because of the consistent way of using metaphors like that.*
>
> TENTH-GRADER LINDA, 2016

THE REMEDIES OR RECOMMENDATIONS

There are actions educational policymakers and leaders in school systems around the nation can take to ensure that the education of Haitian youngsters—as well as other minority students—is no longer under siege, and to give them "this confidence in saying I am Haitian. That's who I am," as Geraldine pleads. It begins with a moral commitment to ensuring that these children—living in the world's wealthiest nation, which is positioned as the leader in human rights—receive a transformative education. That is, an education in which their language, culture, and history become integral components of their instructional experiences. Schools have a responsibility to design and implement programs to address the stigmatization, alienation, resentment, and shame that these youngsters experience and carry from existing in environments where they see their language, culture, and history marginalized and devalued. Schools must be spaces that help these youngsters affirm their identities and become well-adjusted individuals prepared and ready to be in the society.

To achieve this demands adherence to existing legal precedents such as *Brown*, the Elementary and Secondary Education Act of 1965 (in its former or present iteration), the Bilingual Education Act of 1968, and measures such as the 1974 Lau and 1975 Aspira consent decrees which exist to redress inequities, to remedy the poor conditions in which minority children like the Haitians were and are being educated and to provide these youngsters with an education that can respond to their academic, linguistic, and cultural needs.

To remedy the inequities that Haitian children face in public schools, it is imperative to do the following:

1. Create, sustain, and maintain programs at all levels (elementary, middle, and high schools) that leverage the academic, social, linguistic, and cultural strengths of Haitian students and their families.

2. Provide courses in Haitian Creole language and history, music, and art, and courses on the Middle Passage/transatlantic slave experience at all levels.

3. Monitor programs to ensure effective implementation of policies and mandates, as well as adequate staffing.

4. Assure equal access to all education programs, including gifted programs for Haitian Creole–speaking youngsters, and all other instructional and support services.

5. Provide appropriate and sufficient textbooks (English and Haitian Creole), as well as additional instructional materials, or provide for the development of such to support these children's learning.

6. Hire qualified Haitian staff for all programming and services, including bilingual Haitian Creole teachers, guidance counselors, psychologists, speech therapists, social workers, and other support staff who are linguistically and culturally competent.

7. Work collaboratively with institutions of higher education that prepare educators to create and institute courses that expose teacher candidates to Haitian linguistic and cultural practices (*Vodou, rara, vèvè*, etc.) and the Haitian Creole language, as well as to the African diasporan experience (i.e., slavery and colonization; the histories, languages, and cultures of African diasporans; the impact of race and racism on Black and Brown youngsters in society, etc.).

8. Support educational research study initiatives that specifically focus on the Haitian student population.

9. Support the work of community organizations such as the Flanbwayan Haitian Literacy Center, and other entities that advocate for—and provide services that support—the education of Haitian students and their families.

CONCLUSION

Being poor in a rich country can lead to
ill-placed shame, pervasive despair, and anger.

JEAN ANYON, 2005[73]

This chapter was structured to highlight the voices of a group of Haitian youngsters attending the New York City public schools. The youths' reflections on the exclusion of Haitian linguistic and cultural practices as part of their schooling proved illuminating. Their language reveals their fears and apprehensions, as well as their hopes for schools that value and include their Haitian experiences. In other words, these children are envisioning a school system where diversity, equity, and inclusion become norms.

Haitian families and community advocates have long pleaded with the New York City Department of Education and the New York State Education Department to provide Haitian children with linguistically and culturally relevant educational programs and services.[74] The refusal of the system to do so maintains the crippling inequality that began with the horrors of slavery, sustained by the unjust and separatist laws of segregation, and the continuing disregard of *Brown* and other national and local legal mandates. Resistance by the New York City public school system in the twenty-first century to provide Haitian children with an education that includes their language, culture, and history keeps these children's education and identity under siege. Such practice prolongs their academic disengagement and underperformance, maintains their societal exclusion, and potentially relegates them to a life of poverty. Yet America can do better. Let's hope that America listens to the stories of *all* its children.

Chapter 3

FUNDS OF KNOWLEDGE

Culturally Relevant, Culturally Sustaining,
and Reality Pedagogies

Jalene Tamerat

The idea that home and school (or community and school) should not constitute separate worlds, particularly with respect to Black and Brown student populations, is not confined to the funds of knowledge scholarship. Other theories and approaches—for example, culturally relevant pedagogy, culturally sustaining pedagogy, and reality pedagogy—also decry a school–home dynamic that lacks congruence. Several examples from the literature explore the interaction of these domains and urge for their integration. While the funds of knowledge methodology centers on the merging of home and school worlds in a way that is practice oriented, this section also explores the ancillary benefits and other implications of a classroom environment that supports, sustains, and uplifts students' culturally based knowledge and potential for classroom leadership.

Gloria Ladson-Billings, in her seminal work detailing culturally relevant pedagogy, urges the systematic incorporation of student culture as official knowledge in the classroom. Citing a number of studies that similarly link home culture and classroom practice and drawing from her own research,[1] Ladson-Billings's case is made for the building of reciprocal, dynamic relationships between teachers and students as a way to affirm cultural identities, advance critical perspectives, and improve academic outcomes for students of color.[2] While students' home practices, and not culture, are the foci of funds of knowledge pedagogy, some important parallels can be drawn between these two teaching orientations, particularly with regard to their implications for Black and Brown students. There are a number of studies that highlight the potential negative effects of classroom practices that fail to value and incorporate students' culture. For example, POC student dropout, stress, anxiety, and, at times, cultural disaffiliation have been linked with non-inclusive school environments.[3] Additionally, as multicultural education guru Geneva Gay explains, "Double dealing, or being at once highly ethnically affiliated and academically achieving can take a terrible toll on students when the two agendas are not complementary."[4] Incorporating elements of students' out-of-school lives—whether cultural or as funds of knowledge—alleviates the toll of such "double dealing" by bringing needed coherence to POC students' potentially disjointed ethnic and scholarly identities. Funds of knowledge teacher-researcher Norma Gonzalez remarks on the improvements seen in her Mexican American students when their home practices were used to further curricular goals: "I saw high levels of academic engagement and insight in my students who had typically been labeled 'at risk' because of their demographic characteristics. I saw they were as capable of academic success as students from any other background."[5]

Culturally sustaining pedagogy is a response to culturally relevant pedagogy, which, instead of using students' cultural assets for the specific aim of making learning relevant, uses them to prepare students for a pluralistic society. This is important because, according to Django Paris, "It is quite possible to be relevant to something or responsive to it without ensuring its continuing presence in a student's *repertoires of practice*."[6] As Paris recognizes the reality of a multicultural and multilingual present and future (due in large part to the forces of globalization) he sees the difference approach perpetuated by culturally relevant pedagogy as insufficient because it, like the deficit approach, maintains an expectation that students would "lose their heritage and community cultural and linguistic practices if they were to succeed in American schooling."[7]

Christopher Emdin uses reality pedagogy to bring an additional conceptualization of teacher–student role reversal by placing students as repositories of knowledge when it comes to appropriate methods of teaching: "It posits that while the teacher is the person charged with delivering the content, the student is the person who shapes how best to teach that content."[8] Emdin suggests this methodology is particularly useful in classrooms comprised of what he calls *neoindigenous* student populations— that is, students who have been historically marginalized by a dominant power, and who view themselves as separate from those in command. In the American context, neoindigenous is a term that can be used to describe urban youth of color.

Because many American neoindigenous youth are taught by white teachers who do not share (or understand) their backgrounds and may make broad assumptions about who their students are and how they should learn, reality pedagogy brings the student as an *individual* to the center, effectively checking any tendencies to make pedagogical decisions based on what is assumed about students and their cultures. Further, this approach requires an acknowledgement of teacher-held preconceptions and biases that may get in the way of appropriately bringing content to students based on their individual knowledge, experiences, and approaches to learning. By engaging in reality pedagogy, Emdin asserts, the more or less distinct home and school worlds referenced in the work of Ladson-Billings, Paris, and others can be bridged in a powerful way, as teachers and students become collaborative architects of the classroom space.

THIRD SPACE

Paris, in his theoretical framework for explaining culturally sustaining pedagogy, draws from Kris Gutierrez, Patricia Baquedano-Lopez, and Carlos Tejeda, and their development of third space theory.[9] Within education, this is a theory that presents a conceptual space whereby home and school worlds are merged to create new educational understandings and realities.[10] Elizabeth Moje and her coauthors conduct an exploration of this theory that explicitly positions funds of knowledge as a necessary contributor to third space. With a focus on literacy, they argue that "active integration of multiple funds of knowledge and discourse is important to supporting youth in learning."[11] Gutierrez presents the implications of third space pedagogy as particularly important for non-dominant groups because of the binary nature of home and school lives and the "contradictions in and between texts lived and studied, institutions (e.g., the classroom, the academy), sociocultural practices, locally experienced and historically influenced."[12]

The literature depicts three theoretical perspectives on third space.[13] The first locates third space as a geographical site, emphasizing the physical and social places where people come into contact.[14] In an educational setting the classroom can ostensibly serve as the geographical third space where primary (home-based) discourses such as ways of knowing, writing, talking, and reading, merge with secondary discourses that do not have their basis in the home. Homi Bhabha, in another perspective, places third space in a postcolonial context whereby symbols, through discursive processes, undergo transformation to take on new meanings and realities. The third, and perhaps most educationally relevant conceptualization of third space, is the one developed by Gutierrez, Baquedano-Lopez, and Tejeda. Interestingly, in this portrayal, third space is seen less as a site for the development of new ideas and realities, but instead represents a locus for bridging home and school worlds to scaffold and facilitate the learning of academic content.[15] Several studies devoted to the incorporation of third space in academic settings have reported gains in academic engagement and achievement.

The preceding exploration of funds of knowledge–adjacent pedagogical strategies (culturally responsive, culturally sustaining, and reality) and third space theory motivates us to consider the advantages that accompany a leveraging of student assets in favor of more impactful classroom experiences. In a similar way to funds of knowledge pedagogy, students from nondominant and marginalized communities stand to benefit most from these practices as they do not often find themselves in spaces where their unique cultures and skills are upheld or affirmed. Within a classroom environment that serves as a third space for reciprocal, transformative learning, the act of bridging home and school worlds serves as a powerful tool for authentically connecting students with the curriculum.

IMMIGRANT AND IMMIGRANT-ORIGIN STUDENTS

During my time as a classroom teacher in the Boston Public Schools, I consistently worked with immigrant-origin students from diverse backgrounds, several of them hailing from the nations of Haiti and the Dominican Republic. Like immigrant-origin students with connections to any part of the world, each of my Haitian and Dominican American students possessed unique funds of knowledge that I now realize were a direct result of their experiences with migration and/or living and growing up within Haitian- or Dominican-informed home environments. As student funds of knowledge are rooted in experience, and the funds of knowledge of immigrant-origin students are largely informed by the migratory experience in particular, it makes good sense to apply a migration lens to any exploration of the funds of knowledge of Haitian and Dominican American youth.

To provide some context, first-generation immigrants are classified as individuals who were born in one country and migrated to live in another, while second-generation immigrants are those who are not themselves foreign-born, but were born to at least one parent who was born abroad.[16] Together, these groups comprise the roughly 26 percent of school-age children nationally who are of immigrant origin and are receiving their education in US schools. Research on the topic of migration asserts that there are both benefits and challenges associated with the experience of moving from one country to another, and the effects of migration extend to both first-generation and second-generation immigrants.

Immigration can be trauma inducing, whether experienced firsthand or by proxy, when undergone by a parent or close relative.[17] For many immigrant-origin students, this trauma may be rooted in negative experiences in the home country, or in other push factors that led to migration. Many Haitian students and families, for example, have an immigration story with beginnings in the catastrophic earthquake of 2010, while others may have initiated departure from their homeland as a result of economic scarcity, political instability, and/or lack of educational opportunity. Educational opportunity, in particular, seems to serve as a strong motivator for Haitian families as they make the decision to migrate across borders. Many Haitian families view the debilitated Haitian education system as a direct contributor to impenetrable class hierarchies and widespread poverty in that country, and families will often migrate to the US in search of improved access to educational opportunity.[18] This was certainly true for many of the Haitian American students that I had the opportunity to work with over the years.

The act of migration itself can be a source of stress for immigrant and immigrant-origin youth. Within Haitian and Dominican American communities, family separations are common as children will often precede or follow the arrival of their parents to the United States and then reside with family members—sometimes of distant relation—for an extended period of time. A 2002 study led by Carola Suarez-Orozco, Adam Strom, and Rosalinda Larios looked at the immigrant experiences of youth from various parts of the world, including the Dominican Republic, Haiti, China, Mexico, and parts of Central America. They found that children involved in migration to the US tended to be "separated from a parent and siblings for long periods, often years, due to the difficulty in obtaining permanent visas. . . . [Those separated] were more likely to report experiencing depressive symptoms."[19] This was especially true for Dominican youth as they were found to have undergone family separations at a higher rate than other study participants, including those of Haitian descent.

Upon arrival in the host country, immigrants are expected to adapt to unfamiliar cultural norms and oftentimes must acquire a new language as they contend with their departure from the homeland and the social networks that they were once a part of.[20] Unfortunately, these challenging aspects of the acculturative process are compounded by American political discourse that can at times be markedly xenophobic and anti-immigrant. During the Trump presidency, immigrant communities—and in particular, immigrant communities of color—bore the brunt of anti-immigrant sentiment stemming from the Oval Office, dominating the news cycle, and often permeating the K–12 space. During the Trump years, and even today, in US classrooms across the country, immigrant students, both documented and undocumented, as well as immigrant-origin students, have demonstrated heightened levels of anxiety as they and their families contend with threatening insecurities.[21] At and around the time of the 2016 US presidential election, "policy discussions on the status of undocumented immigrants elicited the broadest effects—more than half of all teachers [surveyed] reported students expressed distress related to this issue."[22]

Despite the aforementioned challenges, there are certain school-related benefits associated with migration that extend to immigrant and immigrant-origin students with ties to Haiti and the Dominican Republic. Re-Imagining Migration, an organization dedicated to raising awareness on the topic of migration in US schools, lists: optimism, work ethic, the valorization of education, cohesive families, and bilingual advantages (i.e., perspective-taking, cognitive flexibility) as resiliencies known to be possessed by migrant youth.[23] As Haitian and Dominican American students may either themselves be immigrants or immigrant-adjacent through their familial connections, it is imperative that those charged with their education are not only aware of and responsive to the socioemotional and academic needs that derive from their migration-related challenges, but also retain an assets-based orientation that will allow them to capitalize on student strengths in pursuit of positive educational outcomes. The incorporation of funds of knowledge methodology is a logical means to that end.

THE FUNDS OF KNOWLEDGE OF
HAITIAN AND DOMINICAN AMERICAN STUDENTS

In 2016, I stepped back into the classroom after a three-year hiatus to pursue a doctoral degree, and taught social studies to sixth, seventh, and eighth graders in Boston. Just prior, I had been introduced to funds of knowledge methodology through my scholarship and coursework, and was energized by the idea that I could apply this instructional strategy to forge authentic connections with my students and more effectively connect my students with the content. Because I was new to teaching social studies (I had previously been a middle school science teacher), I figured that this was an opportune time to test out fresh ideas and newly acquired practices, and, because this was also a new school for me, I believed that an application of the funds of knowledge methodology would enable me to better understand the populations that I would be working with while in this new context. At or around this time, I was also engaged in carrying out a qualitative study that, among other things, examined urban teachers' perceptions of student funds of knowledge within their classrooms. By interviewing thirty Boston-area public school teachers, I gained an understanding of not only what these educators considered to be the potential funds of knowledge possessed by their students of Haitian and Dominican descent, but also what they theorized about these groups in a broader sense. Hence, my attempt here to typify the funds of knowledge of Haitian and Dominican immigrant and immigrant-origin youth who reside in and attend K–12 schools in the United States is informed by data from my qualitative study, the (limited) extant research on the funds of knowledge of Haitian and Dominican students, and my own personal reflections while working as a classroom teacher in the Boston Public Schools.

The funds of knowledge of Haitian and Dominican American youth share both similarities and distinctions, which is perhaps unsurprising, given the geographical proximity of the two nations, their historical entanglements, and their cultural differences. One dominant theme that surfaced across my interview data was the idea that young people in both groups were parts of extensive yet complicated family networks within which students spent considerable amounts of time outside of school. Applying the lens of the migratory experience vis-à-vis US visa attainment, we already know that the conception of family for both Haitians and Dominicans extends beyond the nuclear unit, and, in my classroom, it was always understood that "family" often consisted of an amalgam of parents, siblings, grandparents, aunts, uncles, cousins, and/or others who may or may not share one's blood ties.

From my interviews with teachers, it was also evident that the placement of Haitian and Dominican American students within these extensive family networks—and the significant out-of-school time spent with relatives—imparted funds of knowledge that primed them for collaboration and social interaction in the instructional space. The presumed funds of knowledge deriving from these activities varied, but they included skills such as mediation, negotiation, group work, and event planning. For example, Lucy, a teacher in a two-way dual-language immersion school with a majority Latinx population, provided some insight into the specific funds of knowledge that she believed her students gained from their experiences with extended family:

> Many of them are doing quinceañeras. It's the big thing. There's a lot of family trips to the DR. . . . Even if they're not trips, there's a lot of family get-togethers on the weekends. . . . I know that they're usually big gatherings, big family gatherings. There are a lot of personalities to negotiate. [There is also a lot of] getting to know yourself and who you get along with, and then dealing with family drama.

Interviews revealed that many students of Haitian descent were also known to routinely interact with extended family. However for these students, some of whom immigrated to this country in the aftermath of the 2010 Haitian earthquake, the circumstances were a bit different. Noah, a teacher participant at an alternative school with a significant Haitian immigrant population, discussed the unconventional living situations of some of his students, and how many had to endure significant cultural shifts as they migrated from one country to the next, from one set of family members to the next. He reflects:

> The ones from Haiti, their culture is interesting because a lot of them live with people who have come to the United States before them. [They live with] their aunts, or their uncle, or somebody who has been here for a while. They will travel here and live with them. They might have a different culture than the family that they are living with.

Caitlin, a teacher at a different school with a large number of Haitian students, discussed the adaptive (and funds of knowledge–contributing) assets of her students by reflecting on the apparent father-centrism of Haitian families, not necessarily because of particular cultural norms, but because many of these students migrated to live in the United States with their father (who likely migrated first), while the mother remained in Haiti: "Usually the mother does not visit but they do keep up a relationship. I don't know if it's a Skype sort of situation or email or phone calls, but there is relatively frequent contact."

It is also interesting to note that while the literature points to the higher incidence of family separations among Dominican immigrant students, family separations among Haitian immigrant students was a more dominant theme that surfaced from my teacher interviews. Regardless of student ethnic affiliation or national identity, however, I realize that the complication of leaving a parent behind to migrate (or being left by a migrating parent), imparts a degree of adaptability and self-sufficiency that contributes to the development of particular funds of knowledge. Ability to run a household, for example, was an asset that I recognized in my students of Haitian and Dominican descent over the years, and this was confirmed during the year of teaching when I made a specific effort to carry out the funds of knowledge methodology in earnest.

As a fund of knowledge, household management may include the ability to perform routine domestic chores such as dishwashing and meal preparation. However, it is also true that students are occasionally entrusted with responsibilities often reserved for parents: "immigrant parents often may turn to their children when navigating the new society; these children are frequently asked to take on responsibilities beyond their years, including sibling care, translation and advocacy, sometimes undermining parental authority."[24] The fact that many of my former students often acted as intercessors for their parents—or sometimes even acted in loco parentis with regard to their younger siblings—posed some challenges to the creation of a productive school–home dynamic as evidenced by occasional poor homework completion rates and school tardiness. Leveraged effectively however, these funds of knowledge served as powerful scaffolds for accessing and extending what might otherwise have been inaccessible curricula. For example, I found that in-class assignments requiring thoughtful planning, task analysis, and execution were often easier feats for students with household management responsibilities in their out of school time if an explicit connection between those funds of knowledge and the assignment was made. Likewise, students who routinely advocated on behalf of their parents or other family members typically possessed an advantage in the face of persuasive writing tasks.

Evidence shows us that students with ties to the Dominican Republic and Haiti often possess funds of knowledge that derive from living within the transnational space. Dominican American students, in particular, have been known to maintain close ties to their homeland, and live an existence that is "characterized by a constant flow of people in both directions, [giving them] a dual sense of identity, ambivalent attachment to two nations, and a far-flung network of kinship and friendship ties across state frontiers."[25] This transnational identity may be facilitated and maintained through not only frequent return trips to the homeland (often for extended durations) but also through the Internet and media, as well as the "transfer of capital through remittances, goods, and services between the United States and the Dominican Republic."[26]

For both Haitian and Dominican American students, participation in the transnational space supports the retention of native language and culture and bestows a dual frame of reference that supports understanding of life in another country. Interestingly, the dual frame of reference does not seem to be uniquely possessed by individuals with direct ties to the homeland through travel, migration, etc. For example, many of my former Haitian- and Dominican-descended students who were born in the US and who had never set foot in another country were deeply aware of and knowledgeable about the cultural and practical aspects of life in either Haiti or the Dominican Republic (in addition to) the United States, and embodied ways of being that were indicative of a transnational identity. Their understanding of culture, in particular, was impressive, as students portrayed deep knowledge of music and dance styles, like konpa and bachata, and would often refer to either Haiti or the Dominican Republic as "my country." Vivian Louie terms this phenomenon as emotional transnationalism, where the homeland serves as a symbolic place of meaning for youth who are second generation or more, and who do not have direct access to their parents' or ancestors' country of origin.[27]

Still, the experience of physically planting a foot in both worlds—the homeland and the new land—and spending considerable time in each, is a powerful opportunity that contributes directly to the accumulation of funds of knowledge that are rooted in a dual frame of reference. For example, those with the experience of international travel or direct ties to the homeland through migration are often more than just passive observers of the conditions and ways of life abroad; they also have rich immersive experiences that impart a deepened understanding of global issues and varied perspectives. Noah, the teacher in my study from an alternative school, shared how his Haitian immigrant students brought the dual frame of reference to classroom discussions:

> When we look at the world in the class and we try to figure out what is going on, what is wrong with the world, what is right in the world, they [students] can bring a lot of their experiences to it, like living in Port-au-Prince and seeing one-half of the city and the other half of the city in different economic situations. They can bring that experience.

In my own social studies and science classes, the Haitian American and Dominican American dual frames of reference provided logical entry to various topics of instruction, such as population density, microcredit, and climate change. My students with ties to Haiti, for example, could readily share informed perspectives on the consequences of environmental degradation as a result of their observations and lived experiences in deforested areas in Haiti. Too often, however (and I myself have been guilty of this at times), we educators neglect to recognize and capitalize on the transnational experiences of students from countries like Haiti and the Dominican Republic to maximize learning. We fail to consider how these experiences might actually privilege those students with deep connections to the topic of instruction because they and their unique funds of knowledge fly under our radar.

An important exception to this rule is foreign language proficiency. Native language retention is both valued and cultivated within Haitian and Dominican immigrant-origin communities, and maintained proficiency in native languages can serve as symbolic representation of the transnational identity. More often than not—and this was confirmed through my teacher interviews—foreign language–related funds of knowledge are likely to be recognized by educators as an important student asset. However, while teachers in my study were seemingly able to identify the foreign language proficiencies of their Haitian and Dominican American students, they were largely uninformed of the ways that these funds of knowledge might be leveraged to enrich their curriculum in a practical sense.

Admittedly, it can be difficult to conceptualize the ways in which knowledge of Spanish and Haitian Kreyol might be used to extend or enhance a curriculum that is not only delivered in English but deals with topics that are substantively distant from Spanish and Haitian Kreyol. However, one only needs to consider the benefits that are generally associated with being proficient in more than one language to come to a clearer understanding of the relevance of multilingual capabilities vis-à-vis funds of knowledge pedagogy. According to the National Education Association, multilingualism "opens doors to the understandings of other cultures and people who speak those languages."[28] This is an especially important consideration for teachers who incorporate group work and collaboration as part of their educator repertoire, as they likely understand the significance of perspective-taking and encourage that their students consider multiple points of view when working with others. Students who engage with others in Spanish or Haitian Kreyol in their lives at home, and especially those who have been granted access to privileged cultural knowledge through the medium of language, are at a likely advantage in collaborative classroom spaces over their monolingual peers.

In working with my former students, I learned that those with connections to either Haiti or the Dominican Republic were primed to fulfill the obligations of classroom group work not only as a result of their multi-language capabilities but also because of their exposure to communal experiences both at home and abroad. As a cultural norm, collectivism is valued and practiced in both Haitian and Dominican circles. According to Erin Sibley and Kalina Brabeck, collectivism is defined as the "centrality of the interrelatedness of the self to others, with family considered to be an important social resource, and interdependency among family members viewed as paramount."[29] Tapping into Haitian and Dominican students' predilection for collective learning means that teachers would be keen to engage their students in group projects and assignments that require structured peer-to-peer interactions. It also means that a classroom dynamic that prioritizes relationships (both teacher–student and student–student) is both advantageous and necessary.

In this section, I characterize the funds of knowledge possessed by Haitian and Dominican American students as a collective by calling to attention common themes such as family orientation, adaptability, self-sufficiency, transnationalism, multilingualism, and communalism. It is worth noting that there are also potential funds of knowledge possessed by Haitian- and Dominican-descended students that are less likely to extend to both groups, and which serve as evidence of their cultural (and other) distinctions. For example, Josiane Hudicourt-Barnes shows us that among young people of Haitian origin in particular, proficiency in oraliture and argumentation are common funds of knowledge that derive from the distinctly verbal nature of Haitian communicative culture and daily life.[30] The implication here is that a classroom that engages students in acts of storytelling, verbal explications, and oral persuasion within a transformative third space might effectively bridge the school–home gap for Haitian American students. This may or may not be the case for students from Dominican American households.

Admittedly, literature on the funds of knowledge of Haitian and Dominican American students is extremely limited. While this could present a challenge for those seeking rapid insights into the lives of their students, my view is that the lack of formal research on this topic should not be viewed as a considerable detriment since funds of knowledge methodology requires that educators fully step into the investigator/ethnographer role to inquire about the lives and practices of the students and families with whom they directly work. It would be a less than useful endeavor to leverage assumed student funds of knowledge as part of one's practice—even if these generalizations relate to specific groups of students. My fundamental position is that teachers engaging in funds of knowledge pedagogy should always center the people in front of them and bear in mind the fluidity of culture, as practices will inevitably vary from community to community, household to household, and individual to individual, despite some consistencies across groups.

FUNDS OF KNOWLEDGE METHODOLOGY IN PRACTICE

At the start of each school year, like most teachers, I would spend the first week engaging in activities intentionally aimed at building community, teaching and reinforcing classroom protocols and routines, and getting to know the students I would be working with over the course of the year. I would make certain that my process of information gathering about students was always bidirectional; I never wanted to portray myself as someone who was merely concerned with data collection in advancement of some elusive goal. In a classroom setting, sharing personal information can always be tricky as the teacher will want to caution against oversharing, broaching topics that are *too* personal in nature, or simply relaying aspects of their lives that might help to establish *confianza* (trust) but serve no purpose in furthering instruction. Retaining a focus on home-based practices as dictated by funds of knowledge methodology helps to mitigate this, as teachers are not only prompted to model the types of information that they seek from students but also to provide specific insights into their own culturally informed practices (over superficial descriptions of personalities). I have found that an effective means of initiating a year-long process of gathering student funds of knowledge is to directly and formally survey students about their culturally informed home practices. For example, I have in the past implored my students to describe elements of their culture and respond to prompts like the following:

- Walk me through a typical day when you're not in school. List some of your activities (both ones that you enjoy and those that feel more like chores).

- What is something that you know how to do really well that you learned how to do outside of a school setting?

- Who do you live with at home? What activities do the people that you live with engage in on a day-to-day basis? Do you participate in these activities as well?

To model and provide students with relevant examples, I would always make sure to come prepared to share my own responses to these questions. It was also important for me to ensure that those in my classes understood that my intention was to learn as much about them and their families as they were expected to learn about me, and that we would spend considerable time over the course of the school year developing strong relationships amongst ourselves while engaging their families and caretakers in the process.

As a classroom teacher, my endeavors to learn about my Haitian and Dominican American students' lives outside of school were not typically rejected by my students or looked upon with suspicion. I believe that my relative ease in connecting with them may have been aided by the fact that I am a person of color who, although not of Haitian or Latinx heritage, is married to a Haitian American, has visited both Haiti and the Dominican Republic, and is conversant in both Spanish and Haitian Kreyol. Later, as I was conducting interviews with other teachers as part of my research, I learned that educators often felt more successful with making student and family connections when they shared their cultural, ethnic, linguistic, and/or racial backgrounds. It became clear to me that the sharing of personal information between parties was to a large extent mediated by trust that was often imparted through shared aspects of identity. To illustrate, Melissa, a teacher who identified as white, told me: "The parents who have opened up [to me] look like me; they're white. They're the ones that will talk to me a little bit more about their lives."

The dynamic between home and school can be marked by distrust and unfamiliarity, as there are complicating factors that might come into play. For example, when there is an imbalance of power that correlates with race, socioeconomic status, educational attainment, etc., families will not always openly share information regarding their home lives. Additionally—and this is often the case with Haitian and Dominican immigrant families—if one's conceptions of schooling based on personal experience is one in which the teacher is revered as a figure of authority, a reversal of this configuration—where the parent becomes a source of coveted information and knowledge—may be discomforting. For this reason, it is imperative that teachers in their construction of these relationships demonstrate genuine curiosity and respect and are forthcoming with information that provides families with a glimpse into their own lives to help build reciprocity into the relationships that they are attempting to forge.

Having taught for several years in a school where a majority of students were of Chinese origin and where many of the families had limited proficiency in English, I fully understand the challenges associated with carrying out a funds of knowledge ethnography where there is a lack of common language. At my school, language barriers would routinely impede my ability to build relationships with Chinese immigrant families as their English was limited and I had no proficiency in Cantonese. In those instances, I would rely on my students as translators and intermediaries. Though this was not ideal, it did provide me with some insights into their lives outside of school. It also granted me an opportunity to make keen observations of my students as they applied skill with translation as a fund of knowledge.

It is true that shared language between teachers and families would make for an optimal situation, and I advise any teacher engaging in the funds of knowledge methodology with Haitian and Dominican families (or families from any part of the world, really), to attempt to learn even just a few words or phrases in the language that is spoken in their students' homes.

From my own experience and from my interviews with teachers, it became clear to me that language provides access to home lives in ways that might not otherwise be possible, and families will typically appreciate teachers' efforts in this regard. For example, one of the teachers in my study, Lakshmi, an Asian civics teacher of Indian heritage, is not a heritage Spanish speaker herself, but she gained fluency in the language over time. In her interview with me, she shared how her Spanish proficiency allowed her to effectively bridge home and school worlds with the Dominican American families at her school. She also reflected on how her relationships with these families were markedly different from the relationships forged between these same families and some of her non-Spanish-speaking colleagues:

> I think particular to [these] families, something that makes our relationship different is that I do speak Spanish fluently, and I work on a team of teachers where no one else does. So, I am the kind of bridge between school and the home. . . . If there's communication that needs to go either way, it goes through me. . . . It makes parents more vulnerable towards me in a way.

While gaining fluency in a language is, for most, a long-term endeavor and may not be a possibility for all, I urge teachers to also look at how their own life experiences might align (even tangentially) with those of students and families as they try to gather information about students' home lives. For example, it seems that a shared immigrant experience—from virtually any country—could be leveraged in favor of building trust with certain families. Many immigrant and immigrant-origin teachers in my study remarked that students and families who hailed from countries like Haiti and the Dominican Republic were better able to relate to them—and vice versa—because they or

their parents had also immigrated to the United States at one
point in time. Dina, a Barbadian American elementary school
teacher remarked: "More often I see the students' parents [who]
are not from the US. I can relate [to them] because my mom is
not from here. I think I can connect."

In my study, among those who brought up shared connections with immigrant families in their interviews, it was
clear that some teachers believed that country of origin, language, and even racial identity were of little importance in the
establishment of *confianza*. To illustrate this point, Rosa, an
art teacher who hailed from Portugal, shared her experience of
relationship-building through leveraging experiences over racial
kinship:

> So, I immigrated here when I was young. I had a very
> similar story, except I'm white, and obviously that
> changes my experience. . . . But then once they know
> that I also immigrated, and I speak Portuguese, and I
> speak Spanish, they soften up a little bit—the kids and
> the parents.

Similarly, Lakshmi, the middle school teacher whose parents immigrated from India, taught a diverse group of students
that included immigrants from the Dominican Republic and
Haiti, among other countries. In the quote that follows, she
speaks about how she used her experience as a child of immigrants as a gateway to understanding the lives of her students
outside of school:

> We talk a lot about life outside of school because one
> thing that I have in common with a lot of my students,
> not all of them, but a lot of them, is that our parents all

immigrated here. And so there's some things about that experience that are shared regardless of where your parents emigrated from. And so we definitely spend a lot of time talking about the similarities and differences there.

While full adoption of funds of knowledge as a pedagogical strategy would represent a significant undertaking for most teachers, as a methodology and practice, it bears the promise of connecting with and improving instructional outcomes for Haitian- and Dominican-origin students in deep and significant ways. Even for teachers whose cultural, racial, and linguistic backgrounds are distinct from those of their students, the work of establishing relationships through *confianza* and conducting inquiry about the home practices of students and families sets the stage for theorizing, or making broader assumptions, about the funds of knowledge that may subsequently be leveraged for instruction. In classrooms with Haitian and Dominican American students, their teachers would be wise to engage in the funds of knowledge methodology to simultaneously connect students' home and school worlds and make the classroom a space for transformative learning.

Chapter 4

TRIANGULATED IDENTITIES ACROSS BORDERS
Race, Color, and Citizenship

Patrick Sylvain

Much like our DNA informs us about our ancestry and who we are now as a result, our historical legacies are also deposits that chart our contemporary transactions of power. This chapter explores the contemporary exploitation of Haitians in the Dominican Republic (DR) by probing the racial DNA of the two countries. In the twenty-first century, Haitians in the DR find themselves being treated as transient and disposable labor and illegal imposters through political and cultural filters of skin color that harken back to the two countries' slave-driven plantation history of Hispaniola that transformed skin color into a stamp vulnerability and power in the region. This legacy of institutional racism and colorism is a large part of the predicament Haitians face in the DR, where they are denigrated as disposable laborers because they are Black and dark-skinned.

From 1502 until about 1803, the wealth transferred from the island of Hispaniola, comprised of Haiti and the DR, to Spain and France (beginning in 1697 in the case of France) did not simply impoverish the island materially; it also left its devastating mark on the environment and in the form of the genocide of the Indigenous population. Additionally, it plays out in the treatment of certain Haitians as illegitimate subjects in the modern-day politics of migration between Haiti and the DR. Prior to the establishment of the modern Caribbean nation-states of DR and Haiti, and prior to the arrival of Indian and Chinese indentured servants, colonial Hispaniola had three racially distinct groups: the Tainos who welcomed the Spaniards and were subsequently enslaved and killed, the European colonial rulers, and Africans who had been violently captured from various parts of Africa and extorted by the former in the most inhumane ways. Unfortunately, through the intimate as well as forced "mating" between Europeans and Africans, a new crop of mixed folks would give rise to a new form of colorism within plantation slavery, therefore expanding the political framework of racism.

Conquests have long-term consequences. The consequences of a combination of Spanish, French, and American conquest are not only stored in the DNA of the Caribbean, but also manifest themselves on the surface of things. The sociopolitical mutations of color-pricing or indexing that resulted from slavery transformed skin color from a mere matter of the epidermis into sociopolitical stratifications between Blacks and whites as well as among Blacks. Skin color bestowed worth upon individuals with lighter skin, known as "mulattoes," who simultaneously launched a formidable critique of white supremacy and became perpetrators of colorism themselves. As C. L. R. James remarks, "the man of colour who was nearly white despised the man of colour who was only half-white, who in turn despised the man of colour who was only a quarter white, and so on through all the shades."[1] The conquest of Hispaniola begat colorism.

By the time the French and the English arrived in Hispaniola, they lagged far behind the Spanish, who both outnumbered the two new powers and had long prospered as a result of their entry into the island. After 1640, French and British efforts to catch up to Spain resulted in significant demographic shifts through not only large-scale importation of new slaves but also through stealing of slaves from the Spanish territories. Hence, as a result of expediting capital production through competing with Spain, large numbers of Africans died during the Atlantic crossing but their lives were also short on the plantations. By 1700, barely three years after France gained legal control of Saint-Domingue, the western part of the island, over ten thousand slaves were imported to toil in the thriving sugar plantations. Prior to the arrival of the French and British, the Spanish colonies in the Antilles had a monopoly on the slave trade, owing to a special contract system. The logic for having a monopoly, as Frank Moya Pons illustrates, was due to the fact that "King Charles II of Spain was determined to maintain control over the slave market by using a special contract system, called *asiento*."[2] The asiento system, which was dominated by Sevillian merchants, brought to the island a limited number of slaves, leading to a great deal of racial intermixing between slaves and slave owners. When the French and British entered the scene, Spanish control of the slave trade eroded. The French and the British introduced slave-transshipment companies that increased the importation of slaves; as Frank Moya Pons point out, between 1640 and 1700, the French and British changed the demographic of the island significantly.[3] The rapid population changes in French Saint-Domingue gave rise to various forms of inhumane cruelties by the French masters who were eager to accrue wealth. Consequently, sociopolitical contradictions and racial tensions eventually led to the Haitian Revolution (1791–1803) and the subsequent independence from France on January 1, 1804.

Given the overall Caribbean ecology of slave-driven plantation systems, however, the newly formed Haitian state could not escape the crop-based plantation economy. Despite the new country's modest national development vision, Haiti continued to be brutally exploited by France just as it had been prior to national emancipation. After the 1806 civil war, which ensued after the assassination of the nation's founder, Emperor Dessalines, Haiti introduced a tripartite society with different land tenure rules, one of which prohibited foreign whites from ever owning property in Haiti. Freedom from the French did not stop the former slave population along with the descendants of the French as well as the mulattoes (later on the Dominicans) from continuing the practice of sharecropping that turned the Black population into itinerant menial laborers. The systemic culture of exploitation and servitude also created a dominant and non-responsive power structure where poor Haitians are instrumentalized as labor muscles without rights. It is a systematic exploitation that harks back to slavery.

One important feature of worker exploitation was the denial or stripping of workers of their legal forms of identification. The systemic denial of forms of identification allowed for agencies or middlemen such as the Vicini family of the Dominican Republic, who hired cheap labor to work the plantation and so control the Black workers' employment. Unfortunately, the practice of cordoning menial laborers within a confined parameter started in Haiti in 1825 after France militarily demanded Haiti to pay an indemnity to the former French colonial masters for their losses of property. In order to repay France, a permanent peasant class amongst the newly freed slaves was created, and they couldn't leave their assigned plantations without having proper documents. As a result of that practice, Haitians who were not born in the large cities had "peasant" stamped on their birth certificates. Hence, one can read the systemic denial of identification to Haitian subjects as a means of labor exploitation to have survived until this day, used currently as a prominent tool of the exploitation of Haitians in the DR. As Newman narrates, the lack of ID for Haitians means that they "are now stateless, illegal and subject to arrest everywhere in the Dominican Republic, except on the plantation" where they are policed by the plantation security system.[4] Such treatment of Haitians is systemic. The systemic culture of exploitation, and of servitude, shaped not only international relations but also created a local power structure that replicates class relations without regard to the nation's needs. Thus, this chapter navigates the "distant" past in order to better frame the ecology of exploitation and discrimination that now surrounds Haiti in the twenty-first century.

I begin by blankly and sadly admitting that I am from a weak state, and one whose valiant history is no longer revered by most people of the world, because they are operating within the present *cadre* of social realities. Twenty-five years seems remotely far to some, and therefore it might be useless to even venture into two centuries of history. Haiti's power and military history in the world used to be relevant, and Haitians were once very proud of their nation's accomplishments. Certainly, this pride can still be found among Haitians who honor their history and are concerned with the abuses and systematic rejection that Haiti and some of its citizens have gone through and are still experiencing in countries like the Bahamas, Dominican Republic, France, Saint Lucia, and the United States. I have to recognize that Haiti has become one of the most troubling nations in the Americas, and one whose population remains among the poorest and the most neglected. I am reminded of the Antiguan writer, Jamaica Kincaid, who constantly dismisses the accomplishment of the Haitian Revolution because Haiti's present material conditions are so dire. Through my travels and interactions with various individuals, my Haitianness sometimes stirs up emotional responses, from sympathy to fear. Sympathy because of some people's knowledge of Haiti's

history and the pain inflicted upon the country, and fear because of the propaganda that they've been fed about Vodou,
infectious diseases, political dysfunction, and poverty—as if I,
we, are contagious carriers. I always wonder about those poor
Haitians who cannot articulate their own defense in the face of
similar violent affronts to their persons.

Through my travels and my research, I have encountered
various modes of survival that Haitians have employed to remain afloat in countries where being Haitian is akin to being the
devil. Unfortunately, implementing an anti-Haitian ideology
has proven beneficial for politicians in places like the Dominican Republic, the Bahamas, Saint Lucia, and even in Florida.
In places where Haitians encounter violence the attitude of the
state indirectly signals its nationalistic and ethnocentric citizens
to counter Haitians in their own ways. Thus, the recent public
beatings, tortures, dismembering, and killings of Haitians in
the Dominican Republic, although shocking, are nothing new.
Haitians, especially Black Haitians, have been treated as inferior
subjects. Hence, what I have noticed is a form of "passing" or
adaptive citizenship that some Haitians quickly learn through
various forms of cultural sampling. They learn this by acquir-
ing the local culture and parlance relatively quickly in order to
blend in, even though they cannot shed their Black skin. In
the Dominican Republic, the savvy males quickly marry or co-
habitate with very light-skinned Dominicans so their children
can get citizenship. Others Hispanicize their names in order
not to call attention to themselves. In Jamaica, where the social
climate is less hostile, some grow their hair into dreadlocks and
quickly learn to speak Jamaican English. Haitians have become
cultural chameleons in order to navigate this anti-Black and
anti-Haitian world.

As I navigate the complexities of race, color, and citizenship with you, my aim is also to engage in a discussion about

political violence and suffering, as an individual with both academic and real-life understanding of the ways in which unrest, turmoil, and political violence change and shape livelihoods of individuals in oppressive situations. Anti-Haitian sentiments are pervasive in the media and in many of the schools where large number of Haitians reside (New York, New Jersey, Florida, Massachusetts). Amongst teachers and students alike, anti-Haitianism acquires a discourse of backwardness, of incivility, of desperation, of practitioners of obscure African rites that border on cannibalism. Haitians are infantilized; they are rendered *other*, as if they are from a distant past. Whether they are in the DR or the United States, Haitians enter the schools bombarded with ready-made negative markers and uncertainties.

Uncertainty is one of the central features of violence and vulnerability. Uncertainty renders a subject in constant fear and de-essentializes what it means to be free and to be human. In the context of ethnic violence, uncertainty is a very slippery concept and its dynamic range can also be placed in the domain of psychological warfare—the fear of not knowing what the future holds, or the fear of being violently separated from your loved ones. The uncertainty of violence does not lend itself to a universal definition or a systematic approach to analysis; it is simply an element of violence. What it does clarify for me is that Haiti has found itself in a position of uncertainty and vulnerability, and some of its citizens are experiencing multiple manifestations of violence, as they exist in multiple expressions of culture. From the early 1980s with the rise of Haitian boat people perilously entering the United States via Florida; to the violent uprooting of the Duvalier regime in 1986 (Baby Doc), where violence was portrayed in Western media as a common mode of expression; to the 1991 military coup d'état against President Jean-Bertrand Aristide that seemed to further spiral the country into chaos; to the multiple hurricanes in 2008 that devastated many cities and the agricultural plains, which subsequently led to food shortages and protests; and finally to the devastating 2010 earthquake that ultimately exposed Haiti's structural vulnerability, Haitians have been progressively branded not only as the poorest people in the Western Hemisphere, but as undemocratic, backward, and superstitious. With an avalanche of bad press for generations, many Haitian students do not have the language skills or the historical knowledge to contextually explain the root causes of the country's precarity. Additionally, too many teachers and other public servants lack the understanding to fully grasp the complex and complicated background from which Haitian and Dominican students are coming. Conquests and occupations have consequences.

The racialized and hateful construction of Haitians as the undesired other must be carefully analyzed within the context of slavery and the struggle for freedom and citizenship.

THE UNITED STATES
Slavery, Race, and Occupation

The United States has always been a country that positions truths in terms of strict polarities (this or that), and nuances tend to evade constructions of understanding when life has a binary orientation: good and evil, kill or be killed, patriot or traitor, slave or free. In this cultural and historical context, Americans see race in dichotomous terms, black and white, where whiteness is the supposed absence of non-European ancestry. This obsession with dichotomy is successful as a way of establishing easily identifiable phenotypic markers. A good example of this is the way in which the pro-slavery judiciary body of Virginia of the 1630s began slating Africans for distinct treatment. By the time the 1662 act known as *partus sequitur ventrem* (the offspring follows the mother) was enacted into law, stating that "all children born in this country shall be held bond or free only according to the condition of the mother," it not only facilitated the sexual exploitation of female slaves but also guaranteed the longevity of institutional slavery by excluding the position of the father. This law was very different from the laws of the Spanish and the French, where the father could give freedom to his offspring. Hence, color, class, and legitimacy would become the bedrock of contradictions in the French and Spanish colonies. This was more so in the Spanish colonies since the Spaniards did not import their wives or single women willing to become wives in the New World the way the British did.

The American legal and social construction of race for the purposes of racial hierarchy and a reserve pool of free labor was dictated through the blood quantum or the "one-drop rule" that individuals with any amount of racial mixture were legally and socially defined as Black. Hence, from the outset in the United States, race became one of the ways of collectivizing people into a biologically based metaphor projected onto the social, cultural, and legal realms. This is exemplified in the famous 1896 case *Plessy v. Ferguson*. It is worth pointing out that Homer Plessy, an octoroon (one-eighth Black), would have been regarded as white in both Dominican Republic and Haiti. Instead of growing up culturally Black in the US, he would have grown up culturally white in all of the countries in Latin America and the Caribbean.

Today, in the United States, with the upsurge of interracial marriage and the migration of new immigrants from various parts of the world, racial categories and conceptions of race have become much more complex and problematic. Frank Andre Guridy reflects, "Black migrants from the southern United States encountered Afro-Caribbean peoples in northern cities, creating the conditions for unprecedented cross-cultural interaction, even as it also set the stage for intergroup tensions within the context of racism and labor exploitation."[5] The migration of various people of color to northern cities was a direct result of the US empire building that brought forth new economic modalities and racial visions to the region. The term *Latino*, which carries its own cultural and social baggage, adds a new level of racial complexity and identity politics. Cubans, Dominicans, Puerto Ricans, Mexicans, and Brazilians provide a new set of challenges as their color schemes are revealing particularly nuanced ways of self-identifying, while exposing the new dilemma of race in the Americas.

Beginning in the 1950s, Americanizing Latinos who looked European would self-select *white* as their racial category, while those with visible African ancestry would amalgamate into the Black race. Some might be seen as Asian. The US census supported this practice for about fifty years, by publicizing that Latinos could be classified as white, Black, or "other," but not as a race unto themselves. As a result, "Hispanic" remained an ethnic, not a racial category. Individuals of Hispanic ancestry have long had mixed racial identities and classifications. The history of Latin America is characterized by the mixing of European colonizers, native Indigenous groups, and Africans. The result of such a mixture, is a series of hybrids, a pure creolization of diverse hues that can only be color-categorized and not racialized. Whereas in Haiti, despite some relative color mixtures, to be Black is to be free, therefore since 1804 all Haitians regardless of color were classified as Black. To be white in Haiti was to be a foreigner, yet it still carries an upper-class marker. A white person, a *blan,* is the same as the Spanish word *gringo*. A white Haitian is a *blan peyi* (country white), whereas a foreign white is a *blan-blan* (white white). A visibly Black person who was not born in Haiti would still be referred to as a *blan,* a *blan-nwa* (a white-black person) due to his or her attribute as a foreigner.

In 1993, when I worked for PBS *Frontline* as a researcher

and photographer with producer June Cross, an African American with mixed ancestry (biracial is a term that doesn't exist in Haiti), I remember her being totally flabbergasted when General Raoul Cédras had referred to her as a *blan*. This was in 1993, during the first coup d'état against Aristide. As a team, we presented a plethora of skin tones: from dark-skinned Haitians to that of a caramel (*grimo*) hue, to café-au-lait (which June was), to white. Another researcher, a Haitian woman with semi-African features but was visibly white (*blan peyi* or country white), classified herself as white when in the States. According to Raoul Cédras and other Haitians we came across, June Cross was a *blan* and her non-Haitian crew were *blan-blan*. The use of the double adjective *blan* signified their distinction as white people who are also foreigners. June had been used to the absurdity of race in the US, but was completely unprepared for the new categories that were assigned to us in Haiti.

COLORISM AND CLASS IN HAITI

I became aware of color as an identifiable and descriptive categorization by the time I was six years old. Often, instead of knowing names of individuals, color terms and physical attributes were used to identify and label people. In my old middle-class neighborhood of Côte-Plage, it was the adults that gave us the language of color. Doctor Fritz Narcisse, a renowned veterinarian who was already in his late sixties, had a habit of attaching color as an identifier after a person's name, as if your hue was as significant as your last name. It was partly due to Dr. Narcisse's color descriptors that some of us became known as Ti Wouj (red), Kannel (cinnamon), Ti Milat (little mulatto), Tamaren (tamarind), Caramel, Ti Nwa (black), Pèch (peach), Ti Oliv (olive), Oliv Dore (golden olive), Ti Grimo (light skinned), Café-au-Lait, Pistach (peanut), Pistach Griye (roasted peanut), and so on. In our neighborhoods, there were two Reginalds, my cousin Reginald Chatelain and my friend Reginald Azor. It was only customary in a school setting to be called by your last name, which created its own problems because certain last names carry historical weight, some are perceived to be beautiful and modern, while others as common and "peasant-like." Hence, in the intimate setting of a neighborhood, monikers are given as terms of endearment or as reflections of phenotypic descriptors. Reginald Chatelain became known as Ti Milat Bout Siga (mulatto cigar stub) because he was also short in comparison to the other boys his age. Even in his teenage and adult life, although much taller than some of the other boys, Siga remained his intimate nickname as a more personable identifier since there were other mulattoes among our friends. Reginald Azor, however, became known as Kannèl and even after I had lost contact with him for about ten years when I left Haiti for the United States, the moment he called my house in Cambridge and identified himself as Kannèl, his face automatically projected into my mind because of those childhood color descriptors that were assigned to us. It was never about race for us. Even our American friends in the neighborhood (the Walker family) were not racialized but were seen as *blan-blan* because of their foreign attributes. However, Sarah Walker, the youngest daughter, due to her level of acculturation and social fluidity, was regarded as a *blan peyi* (country white).

In my interactions with Haitians and other Black folks throughout the world, the issue of color is a major point of contention. Unfortunately, color has and continues to be correlated with aesthetic value and socioeconomic status. Color also functions on a gradient continuum. Color, according to Christina Sue, "has become salient precisely because racial ancestry is assumed to be constantly constant. In other words, a perceived similarity in racial makeup has heightened the importance of color as a distinction-making marker; color, therefore, has become a proxy for the degree to which an individual represents particular racial poles."[6] In the context of Haiti, the lighter and more educated you are, there is a social assumption of wealth inheritance or access to wealth due to one's social status, especially if it is linked to family standing and legitimacy. Additionally, due to the complete absence of a meritocracy, one's social network becomes essential in terms of social mobility. As one climbs the economic ladder or the ladder of the intellectual elite, marriage is an important consideration, especially for men, as they, more often than not, tend to marry much lighter women in order to secure their social standings. This is almost a prerequisite for Haitian politicians. In the last 121 years since 1900, not one of our presidents has married a darker-skinned woman. Beauty is not simply in the eye of the beholder; beauty is projected and children embrace that projection. For the many years that I have taught in the public schools, the lighter-skinned girls as well as boys were always considered the most desirable. Interestingly, despite the seeming preference for a lighter-skinned partner or friend, Haitians are not intrinsically suffering from a negative self-identification, but are unfortunately caught up in the sociocultural construction of beauty and social mobility, and they inherently enter the racialized economy of beauty without resisting its overall implications.

When I think of the Haitian Revolution of 1804, I certainly think of the promise that it held for enslaved people everywhere and how that newly founded Black nation became not only a beacon for liberty, but also a target of hate toward the very Black bodies who dared to proclaim freedom at the height of white structural supremacy. While freedom was embodied in Haiti, the cancer of race and color and class *appartenance* was already becoming gangrenous from within. The unwavering will of the Blacks contended with a difficult future, and Toussaint L'Ouverture, despite his tragic capture and subsequent death, was one of the greatest revolutionary leaders in history. Had it not been for treason among his ranks, particularly from the insubordinate mulatto General André Rigaud, the outcome of the post-revolutionary war would not have been so rocky.

Following the revolution, color and class conflicts exposed the internal contradictions within the colony. This forced the mulattoes to demand the equal rights that the whites had enjoyed, which then extended to the free Blacks demanding equal rights as well, which eventually led to various groups vying for rights, access to power, and equal representation. Essentially, color and class contradictions as well as political conflicts contributed greatly in undoing the success of the Haitian Revolution.

Jean-Jacques Dessalines, who became the first president and then emperor of Haiti (1804–1806), fought the mulattoes during his consolidation of power and campaign for land reform, leading to his brutal massacre some two years after the January 1804 declaration of independence. It was also Dessaline's determined desire to free the entire island of Hispaniola from slavery. This steered him toward reinforcing the second Treaty of Basel signed by the Spanish Crown in July 1795, ceding Santo Domingo to France in exchange for Catalonia.[7] Legally speaking, in 1801, when Toussaint L'Ouverture took command of the entire island as a French general, he was defending France's interest, but it was because he was a Black commanding officer that the small minority of the Spanish creoles who remained on the island were disturbed. Dessalines, in gathering the spoils of the war, acquired Santo Domingo after it was ceded to France, while also making sure that slavery was abolished on the entire island. However, being governed by Blacks repulsed white creoles and mulattoes on both sides of the island.

From the moment that national independence was declared in 1804 to the United States' occupation of Haiti in July 1915,

Haiti was mired in political power struggles that involved two elite groups demarcated primarily by color but also with minor distinctions in their economic ideologies. Despite the success of the revolution, colonial scars never healed as the pathologies of race domination were secured where boundaries were formed and maintained. Valorization of whiteness persisted in post-revolutionary Haiti, albeit in some small circles of power. David Nicholls's accurate reading asserts:

> While large numbers of mulattoes collaborated with the invaders, the principal resistance in the early years came from black peasant irregulars. Race, the centripetal factor in Haitian politics, took precedence over colour with its centrifugal consequences. The clumsy actions of the Americans, who insisted on treating Haitians of whatever colour as "niggers," contributed to this growing solidarity.[8]

What the American occupation in 1915 concretized was not only the reestablishment of mulattoes as their power brokers but also the exposure of the vulnerable Haitian peasants to extreme violence in Haiti, Cuba, and the Dominican Republic. The cane field immigrants who toiled for American-owned companies would be the ones whose grandchildren are now paperless, or else they were among the thousands deported from Cuba in the 1930s, or who were massacred in the DR in 1937. The consequence of the American occupation was also the establishment of violent dictators who swore allegiance to the US in combating communism and therefore remained against social progress and democracy.

The threat that Haiti presented as a revolutionary antislavery republic in the middle of a global economic system based on plantation slave labor was palpable. However, in the twenty-first century Haiti is no longer seen as a military threat, but as a racial threat. Racism is fully operational and it is now linked to nationalism. As nations are nationalizing their borders or being integrated into the European or North American markets, Haitian presence becomes a nuisance. In the Bahamas, Guadeloupe, the Dominican Republic, Brazil, and the United States, Haitians are being deported and the sociopolitical instability of the country is no longer considered as grounds for granting them asylum. Haitians are seen as pariahs, as impoverished. The present conditions mirror the past in a slightly different context. As Robert May aptly points out, the pre–Civil War southerners "viewed that rebellion and its consequence—the creation of a black republic—in the worst possible light: the very word 'Haiti' evoked images of black slaves devastating property and torturing and murdering their former slaves."[9] Such an outcome certainly could not be allowed beyond Haiti's borders; insurrection was seen as a contagious act, and as such, Haiti had to be contained. Negro rule, or the "Africanization" of power, was the worst nightmare for southern planters.[10] Robert May points out that on February 11, 1854, Judah Benjamin, a Yale-educated lawyer and United States senator for the state of Louisiana claimed "that only slaves could cultivate the tropics and spoke of Haiti's 'decline' since emancipation."[11] The irresistible draw to put Haitians back on the plantations in Cuba or in the Dominican Republic was already in the works. Silvio Torres-Saillant points out how in December 1844, near the conclusion of President John Tyler's administration,

> US Secretary of State John C. Calhoun spoke of the need for the fledgling Dominican state to receive formal recognition from the US, France, and Spain in order to

prevent "the further spread of negro influence in the West Indies." Calhoun, as would many other American statesmen and journalists throughout the nineteenth century, conceived of Dominicans as other than black.[12]

Regardless of the non-racial and pluralistic society that Juan Pablo Duarte envisaged for the Dominican Republic, the existence of plantation slavery depended on a system of economic exploitation with an accompanying racial doctrine. Therefore, John Hogan's concerns regarding the number of people of color present in the makeup of the Dominican population is an extremely relevant point given Dominican President Raphael Trujillo's efforts to whiten the population. Again, Torres-Saillant points out:

> When in 1845 American Agent John Hogan arrived in Santo Domingo with the mandate of assessing the country for an eventual recognition of its independence, he sided with Dominicans in their conflicts with Haitians. As such, he became weary of the predominance of people of African descent in the country. Addressing the Dominican Minister of Foreign Relations Tomás Bobadilla, Hogan wondered whether 'the presence in the Republic of so large a proportion of the coloured race' would weaken the government's efforts to fend off Haitian aggression, Bobadilla assuaged his fears by stating 'that among the Dominicans preoccupations regarding color have never held much sway' and that even former 'slaves have fought and would again fight against the Haitians.' "[13]

CITIZENSHIP, NATIONALISM,
AND POLITICS OF EXCLUSION

"The lighter [one is], the sweeter the sound; and the darker [one is], the tougher the prospect," Lucia Newman concluded in her July 2008 report for Al Jazeera.[14] The situation of Angel Luis Josep, a seventeen-year-old Dominican from the province of San Pedro de Macoris, concretely presents the legacy of anti-Haitian politics that permeates all sectors of the Dominican society, even sports. Because Angel Luis Josep is of Haitian descent, despite having been born in the Dominican Republic, the registry office denied him a birth certificate. A birth certificate would have allowed Josep the chance to fulfill a contract with an American baseball team offering him an advance of US$350,000 to join their club. Due to his lack of identification papers, he couldn't apply for a visa and therefore had to break the contract.

Angel Luis Josep is among hundreds of thousands of Dominicans who have been rendered stateless by the Dominican government. The raison d'état of the Dominican Republic to control its borders as well as applying the rule of law for its internal affairs is not at question. However, the disparity of practices vis-à-vis a targeted group who are forcibly confined to plantation compounds like slaves while their offspring are systematically made into noncitizens in the same way that the children of Blacks in the slavery-held United States were automatically made into slaves as a way of assuring a constant supply of labor is the racially problematic aspect of the Dominican Republic's treatment of the people it deems to have been in "transit" since 1929. In the Dominican Republic, citizenship or the recognition of a person with rights guaranteed by the nation-state is only reserved for certain groups based on racial categories, and unfortunately, this policy of blood nationalism or blood heritage has denationalized individuals who were born and raised within the national borders of the Dominican Republic.

In September 2013, the Supreme Court of the Dominican Republic, citing a "No Rights to Dominican Citizenship" decree, ruled against Dominican-born children and grandchildren of undocumented immigrants, especially Haitians of Black African ancestry. This law, based on a constitutional birthright predicated on blood instead of territory, differs from the laws of most countries around the world. In most parts of the world, birth on a national territory is grounds for citizenship and constitutional rights. The Dominican Republic's restrictions on citizenship have had grave consequences. Its revised constitution of 2010 explicitly prohibited citizenship for foreigners or migrant workers who were "transitory" in the country. This law was first enacted in 1929 under President Vásquez, who signed land transfers and border demarcation lines with Haitian President Louis Borno under the auspices of the United States. As a consequence of the ceding of Haitian land, thousands of Haitians without legal representation found themselves in Spanish-speaking territories. That same year, the economic depression that resulted from a worldwide economic crash forced stock market prices to plummet, severely impacting the cost of sugar. Not surprisingly, this situation resulted in a US-backed Trujillo dictatorship, which orchestrated the 1937 massacre of thousands of Haitian plantation workers in the DR whose labor was no longer needed, and whose skin color was not favored.

In the Americas, a plantation worker (whether under Jim Crow, servitude, cheap labor, *bateys,* or *latifunda*) was never granted the full rights of citizenship, a legacy of the chattel slavery system that dehumanized people of African ancestry. Indeed, plantocracies and colonial structures throughout the world have undermined the human progress of people of African descent. After the former colonies were liberated, their progress was hampered by the law as a major obstacle to their attainment of true meaningful citizenship. Certainly, one could argue in the case of Haiti and the Dominican Republic that former colonial powers have nothing to do with the current quagmire. It is purely an unraveling of national and internal politics. This is true to some extent. When it comes to former colonies, however, the present can never be completely divorced from the past, nor can we overlook the policies of Western countries that have so often infected internal politics of foreign countries with their brand of "racial politics" and favoritism. Consequently, thousands of Dominicans with Haitian ancestry, whose parents were recruited as migrant workers to labor in the large sugar plantations owned by American companies, are now not only facing expulsion for being undocumented, but also their fundamental right of citizenship has been violated by the same system that they labored under and served.

As Western powers champion democracy around the world, in the Caribbean archipelago, democracy is enshrouded in colonial arrangements or operates within non-inclusive political axioms. The market-based needs of the same Western powers who provided the conditions for satisfying consumer demands for low-priced commodities resulted in a large-scale assemblage of extremely cheap and expendable labor. Haitians are one group of people in the Americas who are widely and systematically discriminated against and discarded as disposable migrant laborers. Without a doubt, discrimination is a factor at play in this treatment. Their Blackness, or Africanness, becomes a major discomfort for those who have adopted Eurocentric standards of beauty, civility, and religion.

The hundreds of plantations in both pre-Castro Cuba and Dominican Republic that benefitted from cheap and unrepresented Haitian labor is a direct byproduct of the United States' economic interests that consumed the rights of human beings. Also, note the countless baseball stadiums and hotels as well as the modern subway system in the Dominican Republic that cheap and unprotected Haitian labor helped to construct. The countless Haitian migrant workers that I have spoken to in the DR and upon their return to Haiti have reported the same thing, that they would rather be exploited in Haiti for Haiti's development than to be exploited and treated like dogs in the DR.

The Black body, the Haitian body, not only was denied citizenship, but Haitian bodies formed such a collective of repulsion for the Dominican Eurocentric mindset that masterminded the massacre of 1937—where over twenty-five thousand Haitians were killed after their labor was no longer needed in the sugar plantations and the Trujillo regime claimed that Haitians were preparing to invade the DR—and subsequent killings, hackings, and deportations of Haitians went on with impunity. The weak Haitian state, undergirded by the anti-Black worldview of most of the elite Haitians, did not register complaints against the ongoing suffering of its fellow "citizens." One of Michele Wucker's poignant passages in her book *Why the Cocks Fight* about the 1937 massacre asserts that the "Haitians were transported like cattle to isolated killing grounds, where soldiers slaughtered them at night, carried the corpses to the Atlantic port at Montecristi, and threw the bodies to the sharks. For days, the waves carried uneaten body parts back onto Hispaniola's beaches."[15] In early 2000, when I worked as a public school teacher in Boston, some of my Dominican students used to joke about Haitians who were beaten, humiliated, and killed in various provinces—as if such occurrences were national pastimes.

According to a March 24, 2015, Bloomberg report by Ezra Fieser, a Dominican nurse of Haitian parentage named Anne

Dimanche Saintil, who earned her nursing degree in Santo Domingo and worked at a hospital in the capital, had been recently fired and threatened with deportation. Ms. Saintil is among the 110,000 lives born in the DR of Haitian ancestry and who are now deemed stateless because they are ineligible for citizenship. Ms. Saintil, twenty-seven, reflects: "You're living in the place that's your home, where you grew up, but it's like you are a foreigner, I don't know what my future is here." President Danilo Medina kept his promise to expel thousands of Haitians in waves of deportations that commenced in June 2015, and continued at a slower pace until 2020. President Medina passionately announced his government's intentions during his address to the nation on the commemoration of its independence from Haiti, on February 27, 2015. Between August 2015 to May 2016, according to Amnesty International, more than 150,000 Haitians were deported, and 15 percent of that group claimed to have been born in the DR. Discrimination is and has been a matter of fact in the DR in a similar way to how it openly existed in the United States prior to the passage of the Civil Rights Act.

Started in the 1930s and continuing to this day, the Dominican Republic has pursued a pro-European migratory policy that seeks to lighten its demography. Thus, Haitians became undesirable and are tactically quarantined from the realm of citizenship. As the Dominican Republic grew economically and became a relevant tourist destination, its laws became increasingly pervasive and coercive in order to protect the large-scale post-emancipation system of migratory labor that developed its agricultural industries into modern institutions. By denying citizenship to certain groups, namely Haitians, sugar and construction industries are guaranteed a permanence of cheap, expendable labor. It is worth noting Kimberlé Crenshaw's keen remarks that the "struggle, it seems, is to maintain a contextualized, specified worldview that reflects the experience of blacks."[16]

In the past ninety years, Haitians have been subject to round-ups whenever a Haitian administration attempted to bring up the issue of citizenship for Haitian descendants, or simply to enforce certain trade laws. Indeed, the weakness of the Haitian state renders its people extremely vulnerable.

The unsophistication of Haitians vis-à-vis the law always places them in unfavorable corners when they testify about their reasons for migrating to the Dominican Republic. Despite the semi-coercive nature of their migrations into the Dominican Republic, many of them never cite discriminatory practices in Haiti; instead, they mention the lack of work and extreme poverty as their reasons for migrating. Hence, the protections allotted to political refugees do not apply to Haitians. Certainly, in the United States, Haitians, when compared to Cubans, find themselves in the same quandary.

CONTEXTUALIZING BLACK LIVES
AND STRUCTURAL INJUSTICES

It was in June of 1966, the month and year of my birth, when Stokely Carmichael launched the radical slogan, "Black Power." Carmichael's talk, although a continuation of other ideas that Black people in the colonized world had already put forth in their quests of combating systematic humiliation, repression, and structural injustices, took on a new meaning. The members who attended the Student Nonviolent Coordinating Committee (SNCC) were moved by Carmichael's vision of a broad political and social experimentation that called for a new form of Black liberation and autonomy. This powerful slogan traveled the globe where Blacks' citizenship rights and civil rights under French, British, and Portuguese rule were suppressed. It ushered in new notions of self-defense, self-reliance, self-love, and self-determination. In the Dominican Republic, a form of social consciousness took place, and Blackness, not like the Black Power movement, became acceptable as the country began to experiment with socialism. Unfortunately, in 1963, the US led a coup against Juan Bosch and pushed the country toward military dictatorship. In Haiti, although freed from colonial slavery and direct white rule for a while, Black Power became a symbol of the youth movement who opposed François Duvalier's draconian dictatorship. Meanwhile, on the African continent, some of the countries that were forcibly removing their colonial cloaks adopted a Black Power political agenda that fused socialism as an economic model. Unfortunately, external pressures from capitalist countries with a white ruling superstructure conspired to eliminate or paralyze such movements (e.g., Congo, 1961: Patrice Lumumba's assassination orchestrated by the US and Belgium; Ghana, 1966: a CIA–backed coup against Kwame Nkrumah).

What is abundantly clear throughout the world is that despite the end of the Atlantic slave trade, the abolition of slavery, and the end of colonization by the early 1970s, Black people, on the global scale, have not fully encountered justice, freedom, human dignity, and wholesale progress, even in majority Black countries such as Nigeria, Ghana, Haiti, Jamaica, and Liberia. For the remaining structures of colonialism and the mentalities that maintained the racial hierarchies favoring whiteness are very much woven into the fabrics of most societies that view Blackness in unfavorable terms. Hence, in the case of Blackness in the context of predominantly white societies, where environmental problems have caused maladaptive behaviors, there is nothing more to it than what Martin Luther King Jr., identified as "evidence of racial criminality." This evidence is still very relevant to our current world where Blacks are systematically categorized as other, as a subspecies, and as aberrant. "Crises arising in Northern schools are interpreted as proofs that Negroes are inherently delinquent. The extremists do not recognize that these school problems are symptoms of urban dislocation, rather than expressions of racial deficiency. Criminality and delinquency are not racial; poverty and ignorance breed crime whatever the racial group maybe," said Dr. King.[17] The extremists in the United States, like Rudolph Giuliani, blame criminality by African Americans as an inherent pathology amongst Blacks, and therefore, they need the presence of a militarized police force to control their bodies. In the Dominican Republic, extremists like Consuelo Despradel, a popular right-wing TV journalist who is of Haitian descent, believes that Haitians are pathological subjects, the unwanted criminals who categorically should be expelled.

DISASSOCIATION WITH BLACKNESS AND SEEKING LATERAL INTEGRATION

Some of my Haitian friends and acquaintances who would be considered white by Haitian standards are sometimes assumed to be of Mediterranean or Hispanic heritage in the United States. Regardless of where they may find themselves geographically, those in this group routinely capitalize on their privileged status among Haitians and sometimes others to consciously move up the racial hierarchy—by marrying into whiteness and/ or assuming white-collar professional roles. Their efforts confer not only significant benefits to their quality of life, but also reinforce their distancing from Blackness on the racially based power continuum, where the lowest and least desirable rung is occupied by Blacks. In Haiti, this racialized form of distancing is so pernicious and culturally dilapidating that it has frozen the country in a centuries-long state of dysfunctionality. For

Haitians living abroad, the color divide has weakened any form of collective power that Haitians could have; instead, we remain divided by class, color, political ideology, language, and religious belief.

The act of racial distancing is also common among mixed-race or light-skinned Latinos, particularly Dominicans, who have historically assigned Blackness to Haitians. In the United States, for the most part and although not unique, Dominicans tend to distance themselves from African Americans, which, unfortunately, many Black immigrants do. Some of my Latino/Dominican colleagues and friends do think they are performing a lateral integration into "white" America without losing their full Latino identity, which they see as positive. Whereas culturally integrating into Black America is seen as a downward move and therefore not acceptable to some. In a very revealing post, "Caught in Between: A Dominican Journey into Race," Clayton Rosa writes:

> I was too black for my Latino friends, and too Latino for my black friends—that's how I described the dynamics of my identity at 15 years old. The teenage angst, coupled with confusion, fueled a lack of understanding who I was becoming. I sought out to answer two questions in my college senior thesis: 1) who am I and 2) why. In a society that rejects racial ambiguity and forces people into imagined boxes, racial constructs in the United States are undoubtedly unique.[18]

Indeed, the intersection of racial and social categories that impinges upon national-ethnic identity bleeds disorder onto the makeup of one's existence. Again, reflecting on the crucial moment of racial and cultural awareness, Clayton Rosa adds:

I confronted negative attitudes of blackness firsthand when relatives muttered derogatory racial epithets in Spanish towards my African-American friends. At 10 years old, this confused me since I clearly saw no distinction between them and myself. It's here where these perceptions of blackness are rejected, anything in close proximity to blackness—like Haitians and African-Americans—become alienated and deemed inferior. This is especially telling of the role acculturation plays when new immigrant groups begin integrating into the mainstream.[19]

Within the postcolonial racial matrix, Blackness, and in some circles, Haitianness, implies the undesired attributes of existence within a racialized society. There have been countless immigrants that I have taught, interacted with, and intimately come to know over the years, and while they may have been proud of their roots, they were distinctly aware of the advantages of embracing whiteness without being white. I also notice that among my Latino friends and acquaintances, unlike many Haitians, there is an awareness of the advantages associated with being bicultural and bilingual in the United States where there are vibrant and continuously growing Latino communities. For an Afro-Latino, someone who is visibly Black but speaks Spanish, the reality of dual identities is perhaps a bit more complex as there is a prejudicial categorization that equates Latino to mixed race or being light-skinned. However, as Wendy Roth remarks, "while adopting the cultural behavior of the dominant White group may improve their socioeconomic opportunities, they remain racialized as Latinos—a classification that brings some advantages in terms of affirmative-action considerations, but also many barriers."[20]

On June 13, 2014, Huffington Post Live aired a show hosted by Marc Lamont Hill entitled "Black in the Dominican Republic: Denying Blackness," in which US–based scholars and Dominicans living in the United States participated. The pronouncement of the racial admixture infused the colonial experience in the Americas, specifically on the island of Hispaniola, where "Latino" emerged as a cultural category with a mixed-race distinction, and where Afro-consciousness runs counter. Biany Pérez, a graduate student at Bryn Mawr College of Dominican background and of African ancestry, reveals the dilemma of being Afro-Latina when she states: "I grew up in the South Bronx to Dominican immigrant parents, and I learned that I was Black from my experience here. I grew up in a predominantly African American and Puerto Rican neighborhood, and at the time, in the 1990s, there were no Dominicans where I was living except for us. So, I learned early on that my skin color and my hair were markers of my Blackness."[21] Although, in some segments of the United States and in the Dominican Republic, negative attitudes toward Blackness are positively evolving, there is still major resistance in embracing Blackness as a viable and autonomous human category. The perception of Blackness as a nonviable human quality, or one that implies a strong embodiment of economic assets, is largely due to the fact that dark-skinned Haitians remain in, what Steven Gregory describes as, "the coerced stasis of a slave-like slot in the social division of labor."[22]

The poignancy of Gregory's description of the labor conditions under which Haitians work is critically apropos, both legalistically and socio-scientifically, as it describes the monstrous circumstances of physical labor within the Dominican Republic's agricultural and tourist spaces staffed by cheap and unrepresented Haitian laborers. Given the Dominican Republic's centralized authority within its territorial borders and the various trade agreements signed between Haiti and the DR from 1929 to 1985, it would be entirely impossible for the Dominican government to claim a lack of involvement in the exploitation of Haitian and Haitian-descended migrant workers. One of Marc Lamont Hill's guest scholars, Robin Derby, addressed the issue of denying Blackness within the Dominican Republic in the following way: "Haitians constitute blackness because of the contract labor which brought Haitians in to cut cane, and that associated Haitians as the stigmatized group associated with, you know, a form of labor which was slavery."[23] Slaves were the underdogs, the economic peons of capital. Who would want to be associated with such a class? The colonial stigmas are forever present in the psyche and embedded in the cultural dynamics of twenty-first-century free and postmodern humans.

We need to reconceptualize notions of identity and citizenship in contesting or adapting to national hegemonic influences, reproduction of structures of power if we truly care about establishing justice and human rights for all.

NOTES

Chapter 1: MY EDUCATIONAL WORLD

1. John Dewey, *Experience and Education* (New York: Touchstone Books, 1938), 18.

2. Carola Suárez-Orozco and Marcelo Suárez-Orozco, *Children of Immigration* (Cambridge, MA: Harvard University Press, 2001), 148.

3. Jonathan Cohen, "Social and Emotional Learning Past and Present: A Psychoeducational Dialogue," in *Educating Minds and Hearts,* ed. Jonathan Cohen (New York: Teachers College Press, 1999), 9.

4. Steven Wolk, *A Democratic Classroom* (Portsmouth, NH: Heinemann, 1998), 29.

5. Theresa Perry, " 'I 'on Know Why They Be Trippin': Reflections on the Ebonics Debate," in *The Real Ebonics Debate,* ed. Theresa Perry and Lisa Delpit (Boston: Beacon Press, 1998), 6.

6. Theresa Perry, Claude Steele, and Asa Hilliard III, *Young, Gifted and Black* (Boston: Beacon Press, 2003), 72.

7. Geoffrey Canada, *Reaching Up for Manhood* (Boston: Beacon Press, 1998), 108.

8. Robert L. Fried, *The Passionate Teacher* (Boston: Beacon Press, 1995), 48.

9. Paulo Freire, *Teachers as Cultural Workers* (Boulder, CO: Westview Press, 1998), 22.

10. Jonathan Kozol, *On Being a Teacher* (Chatham, NY: Oneworld, 1993), 20.

11. On the achievement gap, see, for example, Kati Haycock, "The Growing Educational Gap" in *Challenges to Equality: Poverty and Race in America,* ed. Chester Hartman (Armonk, NY: M. E. Sharpe, 2001); Manning Marable, "Focus on the Institutional Barriers" in Hartman, *Challenges to Equality;* Derrick Bell, *Silent Covenants: Brown V. Board of Education and the Unfulfilled Hopes for Racial Reform* (New York: Oxford University Press, 2004). On dropout rates and

college attendance, see, for example, Haycock, "The Growing Educational Gap"; P. Jay Heubert, "High-Stakes Testing: Potential Consequences for Students of Color, English-Language Learners, and Students with Disabilities," in Hartman, *Challenges to Equality*; Bell, *Silent Covenants*.

12. Suárez-Orozco and Suárez-Orozco, *Children of Immigration*, 145–46.

13. Peter R. Breggin and Ginger Ross, *The War Against Children of Color* (Monroe, ME: Common Courage Press, 1998), 168.

14. Breggin and Ross, *The War Against Children of Color*, 177.

15. Robert L. Fried, *The Passionate Teacher*, 27.

Additional References

M. George Fredrickson, *White Supremacy: A Comparative Study in American and South African History* (New York: Oxford University Press, 1981).

Alfred Hall-Quest, "Editorial Foreword," in John Dewey, *Experience & Education* (New York: Touchstone, 1938).

Vivian Gussin Paley, *White Teacher* (1979; repr. Cambridge, MA: Harvard University Press, 1989).

Chapter 2: TELL ALL THE OTHERS OUR STORY

1. "Rara is a popular Haitian linguistic cultural musical performative practice. Rara is music, singing and dancing to drums and *banbou*—an instrument made with pieces of the stem of the bamboo plant—among other Haitian instruments" (Marie Lily Cerat, "Haitian Linguistic and Cultural Practices: Critical Meaning-Making Spaces for Haitian Learners," PhD diss., CUNY, 2017). "Vèvè is a complex Haitian sign system or a set of diagrams. In the Haitian Vodou practice, the diagrams serve to connect the spirit world with its human community of adherents. Vèvè is sometimes inscribed on personal objects (i.e., handkerchiefs, scarves, doorsteps, swords, and the like) and serves the same function as a talisman that protects the person wearing it against danger" (Cerat, "Haitian Linguistic and Cultural Practices").

2. Erik H. Erikson, *Identity, Youth and Crisis* (New York: W. W. Norton, 1968); James E. Marcia, "Identity in Adolescence," in *Handbook of Adolescent Psychology*, ed. J. Adelson (New York: Wiley and Sons, 1980).

3. Jean-Yves Plaisir, "Validating and Integrating Native Language and Cul-

ture in Formal Education: A Plea for a Culturally Relevant Education for Haitian Schoolchildren," *Promoting Child Rights Through Research* 2 (2010): 25–43; Shawn Ginwright, *Black Youth Rising: Activism and Radical Healing in Urban America* (New York: Teachers College Press, 2010); Gloria Ladson-Billings and William Tate, "Toward a Critical Race Theory of Education," in *The Critical Pedagogy Reader*, ed. Antonio Darder, Marta P. Baltodano, and Rodolfo D. Torres (New York: Routledge, 2009), 167–82; Lisa Delpit, *Other People's Children: Cultural Conflict in the Classroom* (New York: New Press, 1995); A. Buttaro, J. Battle, and A. Pastrana, "The Aspiration-Attainment Gap: Black Students and Education," *Journal of Negro Education* 79, no. 4 (2010): 488–502.

4. Gary Orfield, John Kucsera, and Genevieve Siegel-Hawley, *E Pluribus . . . Separation: Deepening Double Segregation for More Students* (Los Angeles: Civil Rights Project/Derechos Civiles, University of California, 2012).

5. Segregation was the implementation of the "separate but equal" laws, following the 1896 US Supreme Court decision in *Plessy v. Ferguson*. The "separate but equal" laws—also referred to as the Jim Crow laws—mandated the separation of Blacks and whites in all areas of American society. These laws would not be changed until 1954, when the National Association for the Advancement of Colored People (NAACP) challenged them in court, decrying the poor conditions in which Black children were educated. With the 1954 *Brown v. Board of Education of Topeka* decision, the US Supreme Court annulled the laws of Plessy, and instructed the integration of Blacks in all areas. Education became the first site to be impacted by *Brown*.

6. Haiti is the first independent nation in the Western Hemisphere created by former slaves. In 1804, following their anti-slavery struggle and revolutionary war against colonial France, the Haitians established their new free country. Today, Haiti shares the second-largest island in the Caribbean with the Dominican Republic. For the experiences of Haitians in recent history, see François Pierre-Louis, "A Long Journey from Protest to Incorporations: The Political Development of Haitians in New York City," *Journal of Haitian Studies* 17, no. 2 (2011): 52–72; Bernard Diederich, *The Price of Blood: History of Repression and Rebellion in Haiti Under Dr. François Duvalier* (Princeton, NJ: Markus Wiener Publishers, 2011); Alex Stepick, *Pride Against Prejudice: Haitians in the United States* (Needham Heights, MA: Allyn and Bacon, 1998); Michel S. Laguerre, *American Odyssey: Haitians in New York City* (Ithaca, NY: Cornell University Press, 1984).

7. Yearbook of Immigration Statistics, Office of Immigration Statistics, 2017, US Department of Homeland Security. The half million figure only includes individuals who obtained permanent residency. The number of undocumented people is not factored in.

8. François Pierre-Louis, "A Long Journey from Protest to Incorporations," 52–72; Georges Fouron, "The History of Haiti in Brief," in *The Haitian Creole Language: History, Structure, Use and Education*, ed. Arthur K. Spears and Carole M. Berotte Joseph (New York: Lexington Books, 2010), 23–54; Patrick Bellegarde-Smith, *Haiti: The Breached Citadel* (Toronto: Canadian Scholars Press, 2004); Alex Dupuy, *Haiti in the New World Order: The Limits of the Democratic Revolution* (Boulder, CO: Westview Press, 1997); Laguerre, *American Odyssey*.

9. Religious freedom was never threatened under the Duvaliers.

10. The Haitian economy began to deteriorate immediately after the country's independence in 1804. "Haiti was viewed as an insult to most whites who believed in the natural inferiority of blacks. Consequently, to preserve the status quo, Western imperialist powers quarantined Haiti within the international community as if it were a plague" (Georges Fouron, "The History of Haiti in Brief," 30). Moreover, the indemnity of 150 million francs imposed by France on Haiti in order to recognize its independence further destroyed the economy of the new nation—once known as the most profitable colony in the Antilles (Laurent Dubois, *Haiti: The Aftershocks of History* [New York: Metropolitan Books, 2012]).

11. Diederich, *The Price of Blood*; Patrick Lemoine, *Fort Dimanche, Fort-La-Mort* (Bloomington, IN: Trafford Publishing, 1996); Elizabeth Abbott, *Haiti: The Duvaliers and Their Legacy* (New York: McGraw-Hill, 1988).

12. Carole J. Berotte Joseph, "Haitians in the US: Language, Politics, and Education," in Spears and Joseph, *The Haitian Creole Language*; Laguerre, *American Odyssey*.

13. Duvalier loyalists like army general Jacques Gracia kept the authoritarian system in place. The Duvalierists continued to govern with impunity. Many more people were made to disappear, and countless others killed (Elizabeth Abbott, *Haiti*; Lemoine, *Fort Dimanche, Fort-La-Mort*; Nancy Gordon Heinl and Robert Debs Heinl, *Written in Blood: The Story of the Haitian People, 1492–1971* (Boston: Houghton Mifflin, 1978).

14. Many Haitians entered the United States on visitors' visas, while others sought refuge in the neighboring Dominican Republic, surrounding Caribbean island nations, French-speaking Montréal in Canada, and a few West African countries. 2017 Yearbook of Immigration Statistics, Office of Immigration Statistics.

15. Stepick, *Pride Against Prejudice*; Laguerre, *American Odyssey*.

16. Jane Guskin and David L. Wilson note: "Some 800,000 Cubans immigrated to the United States between 1960 and 1980. . . . But they were able to come because the U.S. government actively encouraged Cubans to immigrate. From 1959 to 1961, about 125,000 Cubans arrived in the United States. The U.S. Coast Guard did nothing to stop them from entering the country." Guskin and Wilson, *The Politics of Immigration: Questions and Answers*, 2nd ed. (New York: New York University Press, 2017, 52–53).

17. Guskin and Wilson, *The Politics of Immigration*; Naomi Paik, "Testifying to Rightlessness: Haitian Refugees Speaking from Guantánamo," *Social Text* 28, no. 3 (2010): 39–65; Brandt Goldstein, *Storming the Court: How a Band of Yale Law Students Sued the President and Won* (New York: Scribner, 2005); Stepick, *Pride Against Prejudice*; Laguerre, *American Odyssey*.

18. Laguerre, *American Odyssey*, 12.

19. On February 7, 1986, Haitians of all ages in Brooklyn, New York, filled Eastern Parkway to celebrate the departure of Jean Claude (Baby Doc) Duvalier and the end of the Duvalierist dictatorship. The father and son tyrants ruled Haiti with an iron hand from 1957 to 1986.

20. In Haiti, many people believe that there exists an herbal and animal potion that, if given to someone, can turn them into a will-less and speechless person, a *zonbi*. According to Claudine Michel and Patrick Bellegarde-Smith, "Haitian Vodou seems to be a compendium of a deliberate amalgam of Dahomean traditions, those of the Kongo basin and surrounding ethnic nations in both West and Central Africa. But the origins of Vodou lie in Dahomey (present-day Benin), either because that population provided a critical mass to that of colonial Saint-Domingue over a historical period of time or because Dahomean tradition offered a theological sophistication found throughout that region of Africa in Yoruba, Dogon, Dagara peoples and others." Michel and Bellegarde-Smith, *Haitian Vodou: Spirit, Myth and Reality* (Bloomington: Indiana University Press, 2006), xix.

21. Jean Bertrand Aristide was a young priest who came to prominence in the early 1980s for his anti-Duvalier sermons. Using his church pulpit, he criticized the dictatorship for its human rights abuses and exploitation as well as neglect of the Haitian people. His pointed sermons delivered in Haitian Creole in one of the poorest parishes of Port-au-Prince gained him huge popularity. Four years after the fall of Jean Claude (Baby Doc) Duvalier, Aristide would run for, and win, the Haitian presidency in a landslide to become the first democratically elected president of Haiti in modern history. Both of his presidential mandates were cut short by coups d'état. In 1991, a year into his first term, he was deposed by the Haitian military, but returned with the assistance of the United States three years later to complete his term. He ran and won the presidency for a second time in 2001. Three years into that second term he was ousted again. Aristide has since returned to Haiti to live as a private citizen. He teaches at the university he helped to establish in Tabarre, a suburb of Port-au-Prince.

22. In December 1992, I took a leave of absence from my position as a parent counselor with the Day Care Council of New York to serve as a Creole-language specialist with the US Department of Justice Immigration and Naturalization Service to interpret for Haitian asylum seekers encamped on Guantánamo. On that first trip, I spent two and half months on the Guantánamo US Naval Base. Guantánamo is located in the southeast of Cuba, although it has been controlled by the United States since the Spanish–American War at the turn of the twentieth century; Goldstein, *Storming the Court*, 19.

23. Koh's co-teacher at the Yale Lowenstein Law Clinic was Michael Ratner, a human rights lawyer. With lawyers Ira Kurzban and Cheryl Little of the Haitian Centers in Miami, the legal team launched the historic court battle.

24. Goldstein, *Storming the Court*; Paik, "Testifying to Rightlessness."

25. To limit the length of the historical timeframe, I only note here that Aristide eventually returned from exile to finish his first term. He ran again five years later, was reelected, and took office in February 2001. He suffered a second coup d'état, in 2004, and was sent back in exile. In 2011, he returned to Haiti, and currently lives in the country as a private citizen.

26. Haiti is indeed the poorest country in the Western Hemisphere. However, it needs to be noted that the former French colony of Saint-Domingue was considered "the most profitable bit of land in

the world" for its colonial ruler France (Dubois, *Haiti*, 4). Economic isolation of Haiti following its independence by many European countries and the United States contributed to impoverishing Haiti. Thus, there is an important history of the pauperization of Haiti that should never be ignored.

27. Mark Schuller, *Killing with Kindness: Haiti, International Aid, and NGOs* (New Brunswick, NJ: Rutgers University Press, 2012); Dubois, *Haiti*.

28. Myriam Merlet, Magalie Marcelin, and Anne Marie Coriolan, three feminist leaders whose advocacy work on behalf of Haitian women and girls was helping to transform Haiti into a more equitable space, perished in the quake. Myriam Chancy, *From Sugar to Revolution: Women's Visions of Haiti, Cuba, and the Dominican Republic* (Waterloo, ONT: Wilfrid Laurier University Press, 2012).

29. The devastated south is still reeling to recover.

30. Haiti was a former colony of Spain and France and contributed to creating the wealth of these two colonial countries. While it is difficult to avoid the line, "the poorest country in the Western Hemisphere," it is important to remind readers that Haiti was, and is still, a rich land. However, the continuous exploitation by the former colonials and neo-colonials further contributes to the underdevelopment of the Haitian nation.

31. See the *New York Daily News* article "Enraged President Trump Reportedly Said All Haitians Have AIDS, Nigerians Own Huts at Immigration Meeting" by Denis Slattery on December 23, 2017; Michael D. Shear and Julie Hirschfeld Davis, "Stoking Fears, Trump Defied Bureaucracy to Advance Immigration Agenda" *New York Times*, December 23, 2017; Eli Watkins, "WH Denies NYT Report Claiming Trump Said Haitian Immigrants 'all have AIDS,'" CNN, December 24, 2017; or Joel Dreyfuss, "No, President Trump, We Haitians Don't All Have AIDS," *Washington Post*, op-ed, December 28, 2017. The meeting included discussion on the fate of individuals with temporary protective status (TPS), an immigration category granted to people whose countries are ravaged by wars and/or natural disasters, including Haiti.

32. Haitian immigrants in the United States who were following the news about civil unrest in Haiti at the time of the departure of Jean Claude (Baby Doc) Duvalier in February 1986 can recall Jeane D. Kirkpatrick, a political scientist and US diplomat in the Ronald Reagan administration, referring to Haiti as "a basket case" on national television. And

that was not even the first time a high-ranking US official was known
to use racist and derogatory language to describe Haiti or its people.

33. From 1998 to 2001, and from 2003 to 2010, I worked as a resource
specialist for the now defunct Haitian Bilingual Education Technical
Assistance Center (HABETAC), housed at the City College of New
York of the City University of New York. Haitian students attending
the college often visited the office, and employees of the HABETAC
supported and attended activities held by the Haitian Students Association (HASA) on campus. It was during those years that I learned
the acronym *HU* for Haitian Undercover from the Haitian students
attending the college. The HABETAC deliverables also entailed working with New York City high schools that had bilingual Haitian Creole
programs. I also later heard the term used by some Haitian high school
students in the New York City public schools.

34. For news of the FDA's policy announcement, see Bruce Lambert,
"Now, No Haitians Can Donate Blood," *New York Times*, March 14,
1990. See also Carl Lindskoog, *Detain and Punish: Haitian Refugees
and the Rise of the World's Largest Immigration Detention System* (Gainesville: University of Florida Press, 2018); Goldstein, *Storming the Court*;
Stepick, *Pride Against Prejudice*.

35. On April 20, 1990, thousands of Haitian men, women, and children,
as well as their allies, walked across the Brooklyn Bridge to decry and
denounce the racist policy of the FDA and CDC in one of the most
historic and largest demonstrations in New York, and the United States.
The public pressure forced the FDA and CDC to cave in, offer a public
apology, and rescind the policy. But the damage was done; the dark
and tainted historical moment as well as the shame remained.

36. The United States ban on HIV-positive foreigners was introduced
in 1987 under the Reagan administration and lasted for over twenty
years. It affected tourists and foreigners seeking visas to enter the
United States.

37. Goldstein, *Storming the Court*, 56–58.

38. Stepick, *Pride Against Prejudice*.

39. Flore Zéphir, "The Languages of Haitians and the History of Creole:
Haitian and Its Diaspora," in Spears and Joseph, *The Haitian Creole
Language*; Iv Dejan, *Yon lekòl tèt anba nan yon peyi tèt anba* (Port-au-
Prince: Imprimerie Henri Deschamps, 2006); Michel DeGraff, "Lin-
guists' Most Dangerous Myth: The Fallacy of Creole Exceptionalism,"
Language in Society 34 (2005): 533–91.

40. Stepick, *Pride Against Prejudice*, 1.

41. Stepick, *Pride Against Prejudice*.

42. Goldstein, *Storming the Court*.

43. Randy Shilts, *And the Band Played On* (New York: St. Martin's Press, 1987).

44. Erikson, *Identity, Youth and Crisis*; James E. Marcia, "Identity in Adolescence," in *Handbook of Adolescent Psychology*, ed. Joseph Adelson (New York: Wiley and Sons, 1980); Elisabetta Crocetti, Rasa Erentaité, and Rita Zukauskiené, "Identity Styles, Positive Youth Development, and Civic Engagement in Adolescence," *Journal Youth Adolescence* 43 (2014): 1818–28; Michael D. Berzonsky, "Identity Style: Conceptualization and Measurement," *Journal of Adolescent Research in Personality* 4 (1989): 268–82; Michael D. Berzonsky, "Identity Style and Well-Being: Does Commitment Matter?," *Identity: An International Journal of Theory and Research* 3 (2003): 131–42.

45. One fairly well-known example is how many in the US German community altered and/or anglicized the spelling of their surnames to weather anti-German sentiment as xenophobia against them increased during World War II.

46. Stepick, *Pride Against Prejudice*.

47. Stepick, *Pride Against Prejudice*.

48. Geraldine, interview with author, 2016.

49. Vasiliki Fouka, "How Do Immigrants Respond to Discrimination? The Case of Germans in the US During World War I," *American Political Science Review* 113, no. 2 (2019): 405–22; Patricia Michaelis, "Crisis of Loyalty: Examples of Anti-German Sentiment from Kansas Memory," *Kansas History* 40, no. 1 (2017): 20–29; George Wieland, "Americanization: Hastened by Hate?" *Michigan History Magazine* (July–August 2010): 54. "In the early years of the twentieth century, Germans in Ann Arbor proudly proclaimed their ethnic origin in the establishment of their own schools, churches, and businesses. Then war erupted in Europe, forcing many to hide their heritage or even renounce it."

50. Goldstein, *Storming the Court*, 56.

51. The scope of this document limits a thorough discussion on being Black in America, which carries its own weight. In fact, the Haitian youth that participated in the focus groups and ethnographic interviews brought up the Black Lives Matter movement. They identify with it and recognize that they are part of the US Black community—

albeit indistinguishable from other Black peers—and are viewed and victimized by the police in the same way as all other Black persons in the country. Recall the Brooklyn graffiti, "Haitians = Niggers with AIDS," cited by Goldstein in *Storming the Court*; Stepick, *Pride Against Prejudice*.

52. Goldstein, *Storming the Court*.

53. Jim Cummins, *Negotiating Identities: Education for Empowerment in a Diverse Society* (Los Angeles: California Association for Bilingual Education, 2001), 3.

54. Ta-Nehisi Coates, *Between the World and Me* (New York: Spiegel and Grau, 2015), 25–27.

55. John Kucsera and Gary Orfield, *New York State's Extreme School Segregation: Inequality, Inaction, and a Damaged Future* (Los Angeles: Civil Rights Project/Derechos Civiles, University of California, 2014).

56. Jean Anyon, *Radical Possibilities: Public Policy, Urban Education, and a New Social Movement* (New York: Routledge, 2005); Ofelia García, *Bilingual Education in the 21st Century: A Global Perspective* (Malden, MA: Wiley-Blackwell, 2009); Anthony Buttaro Jr., Juan Battle, and Antonio (Jay) Pastrana Jr., "The Aspiration–Attainment Gap: Black Students and Education," *Journal of Negro Education* 79, no. 4 (Fall 2010): 488–502.

57. New York City Department of Education, Division of English Language Learners and Support, *English Language Learner Demographics Report for the 2016–17 School Year*. The one bilingual high school program is located at Clara Barton High School in Brooklyn, and the two for elementary and middle-school levels are at P.S. 189K, the Bilingual Center (K-8), and P.S. 276K.

58. Flanbwayan Haitian Literacy Project, *Going to School and Not Getting an Education*, a community report on Haitian newcomer immigrant students at Tilden High School in Brooklyn, New York, 2011, 11.

59. Flanbwayan Haitian Literacy Project, *Going to School and Not Getting an Education*, 3.

60. Flanbwayan report, *Left Out: The Struggle of Newly Arrived Haitian Immigrant Youth Enrolling in New York City High Schools Through Family Welcome Centers*, 2019; Marie Lily Cerat, "Myths and Realities: A History of Haitian Creole Language Programs in New York City," *Journal of Haitian Studies* 17, no. 2 (2011): 73–91; Joseph, "Haitians in the US."

61. New York City Civil Court deposition given by Multicultural Education Training and Advocacy, META, 1996.

62. Tove Skuttnab-Kangas, "Language Policy and Linguistic Human Rights," in *An Introduction to Language Policy Theory and Method*, ed. Thomas Ricento (Malden, MA: Wiley-Blackwell, 2006), 273–91.

63. Plaisir, "Validating and Integrating Native Language and Culture in Formal Education"; Ladson-Billings and Tate, "Toward a Critical Race Theory of Education"; Delpit, *Other People's Children*; Ginwright, *Black Youth Rising*; Anthony Buttaro Jr., Juan Battle, and Antonio (Jay) Pastrana Jr., "The Aspiration–Attainment Gap; Carola Suárez-Orozco, Marcelo M. Suárez-Orozco, and Irina Todorova, *Learning a New Land: Immigrant Students in American Society* (Cambridge, MA: Belknap Press of Harvard University Press, 2008); Flanbwayan, *Going to School and Not Getting an Education*.

64. Coates, *Between the World and Me*, 25–26.

65. Ginwright, *Black Youth Rising*.

66. James W. Loewen, *Lies My Teacher Told Me* (New York: Simon and Schuster, 2007).

67. Ginwright, *Black Youth Rising*.

68. Delpit, *Other People's Children*, 177.

69. The Venezuelan Simón José Antonio de la Santísima Trinidad Bolívar y Palacios Ponte-Andrade y Blanco (July 24, 1783–December 17, 1830), known as Simón Bolívar or El Libertador, went to Haiti in 1815, following an assassination attempt on his life. The Haitian leader Alexandre Petion supplied him with soldiers and military ammunitions to support his fight to liberate Venezuela, Bolivia, Colombia, Ecuador, Peru, and Panama from colonial Spain.

70. In 2015, Rodneyse Bichotte became assemblyperson for the 42nd Assembly District in New York. She was the first Haitian American woman from New York City to be elected to the state legislature.

71. Haitians have a long history and presence in this country. Historical records show that some eight hundred Haitians served as volunteer soldiers in colonial America's war for independence at the Battle of Savannah in 1779. Pierre Toussaint, a Haitian slave who accompanied his master, a plantation owner named Bérard, fleeing the Haitian Revolution, came to New York City in 1787 and became a well-known hairdresser in the city. Pierre donated a lot to charity, including funds that went toward building Saint Patrick's Cathedral. Today, there are

many Haitians working in all fields in the city from education to health care to politics. Jacques Jiha is serving as the current New York City Commissioner of Finance. Patrick Gaspard, the current president of the Open Society Foundations, also had an illustrious career in government. Judge Dweynie Paul became the first Haitian American woman to be elected a civil court judge in New York City.

72. Henry Louis Gates Jr., *Black in Latin America* (New York: New York University Press, 2011); Laurent Dubois, *Avengers of the New World* (Cambridge, MA: Belknap Press of Harvard University Press, 2004); Susan Buck-Morss, *Hegel, Haiti and Universal History* (Pittsburgh: University of Pittsburgh Press, 2009).

73. Jean Anyon, *Radical Possibilities: Public Policy, Urban Education and a New Social Movement* (New York: Routledge, 2005).

74. In 1996, the New York Haitian community with the assistance of the Boston-based Multicultural Education Training and Advocacy (META) initiated a court case against the then New York City Board of Education (currently the New York City Department of Education) and the New York State Education Department, alleging educational neglect of Haitian children.

Chapter 3: FUNDS OF KNOWLEDGE

1. Kathryn Hu-Pei Au and Cathie Jordan, "Teaching Reading to Hawaiian Children: Finding a Culturally Appropriate Solution," in *Culture and the Bilingual Classroom: Studies in Classroom Ethnography*, ed. Henry T. Trueba, Grace Pung Guthrie, and Kathryn Hu-Pei Au (Rowley, MA: Newbury House, 1981), 139–52; Gerald Mohatt and Frederick Erickson, "Cultural Differences in Teaching Styles in an Odawa School: A Sociolinguistic Approach," in Trueba, Guthrie, and Hu-Pei Au, *Culture and the Bilingual Classroom*, 105.

2. Gloria Ladson-Billings, "Toward a Theory of Culturally Relevant Pedagogy," *American Educational Research Journal* 32, no. 3 (1995): 465–91.

3. Donna Deyhle, "Navajo Youth and Anglo Racism: Cultural Integrity and Resistance," *Harvard Educational Review* 65, no. 3 (1995): 403–45; P. N. Kiang and J. Kaplan, "Race/Space Relations in School," *NABE News* 17, no. 6 (1994).

4. Geneva Gay, *Culturally Responsive Teaching: Theory, Research, and Practice* (New York: Teachers College Press, 2000), 19.

5. Norma González, Luis C. Moll, and Cathy Amanti, *Funds of Knowledge: Theorizing Practices in Households, Communities, and Classrooms* (New York: Routledge, 2005), 7.

6. Django Paris, "Culturally Sustaining Pedagogy: A Needed Change in Stance, Terminology, and Practice," *Educational Researcher* 41, no. 3 (2012): 95, doi:10.3102/0013189x12441244.

7. Paris, "Culturally Sustaining Pedagogy," 94.

8. Christopher Emdin, *For White Folks Who Teach in the Hood—and the Rest of Y'all Too: Reality Pedagogy and Urban Education* (Boston: Beacon Press, 2016), 27.

9. Kris D. Gutiérrez, Patricia Baquedano-Lopez, and Carlos Tejeda, "Rethinking Diversity: Hybridity and Hybrid Language Practices in the Third Space," *Mind, Culture, and Activity* 6 (1999): 286–303.

10. Gutiérrez, Baquedano-Lopez, and Tejeda, "Rethinking Diversity"; Elizabeth Burr Moje et al., "Working Toward Third Space in Content Area Literacy: An Examination of Everyday Funds of Knowledge and Discourse," *Reading Research Quarterly* 39, no. 1 (2004): 38–70, doi:10.1598/rrq.39.1.4; Paris, "Culturally Sustaining Pedagogy."

11. Moje et al., "Working toward Third Space in Content Area Literacy," 41.

12. Kris D. Gutiérrez, "Developing a Sociocritical Literacy in the Third Space," *Reading Research Quarterly* 43, no. 2 (2008): 149, doi:10.1598/rrq.43.2.3.

13. Moje et al., "Working toward Third Space in Content Area Literacy."

14. Edward W. Soja. *Thirdspace: Expanding the Geographical Imagination* (Oxford: Blackwell, 1996).

15. Moje et al., "Working toward Third Space in Content Area Literacy."

16. Carola Suárez-Orozco, Adam Strom, and Rosalinda Larios, "A Culturally Responsive Approach to Understanding Immigrant Origin Children," *Re-Imagining Migration*, https://reimaginingmigration.org/a-culturally-responsive-guide-to-understanding-immigrant-origin-children.

17. Suárez-Orozco, Strom, and Larios, "A Culturally Responsive Approach."

18. Neporcha Cone, Cory Buxton, Okhee Lee, and Margarette Mahotiere, "Negotiating a Sense of Identity in a Foreign Land," *Urban Education* 49, no. 3 (2013): 263–96, https://doi.org/10.1177/0042085913478619.

19. Suárez-Orozco, Strom, and Larios, "A Culturally Responsive Approach."

20. Suárez-Orosco, Strom, and Larios, "A Culturally Responsive Approach," 26.

21. John Rogers, "Teaching and Learning in the Age of Trump: Increasing Stress and Hostility in America's High Schools," *IDEA* (2017): 28, https://idea.gseis.ucla.edu/publications/teaching-and-learning-in-age -of-trump.

22. Rogers, "Teaching and Learning in the Age of Trump," 28.

23. Re-Imagining Migration Fellows presentation, Re-Imagining Migration Seminar, Washington, DC, June 27, 2019.

24. Suárez-Orosco, Strom, and Larios, "A Culturally Responsive Approach," 26.

25. Jorge Duany, *Quisqueya on the Hudson: The Transnational Identity of Dominicans in Washington Heights* (New York: CUNY Dominican Studies Institute, 1994), 2.

26. González and Rubenstein-Ávila, *The Policies of Immigrant Education: Multi-National Perspectives,* 571.

27. Vivian Louie, "Second-Generation Pessimism and Optimism: How Chinese and Dominicans Understand Education and Mobility through Ethnic and Transnational Orientations," *International Migration Review* 40, no. 3 (2006): 537–72, https://doi.org/10.1111/j.1747-7379 .2006.00035.x.

28. National Education Association, "Global Competence Is a 21st Century Imperative: An NEA Policy Brief," National Center for Educational Statistics (2010).

29. Erin Sibley and Kalina Brabeck, "Latino Immigrant Students' School Experiences in the United States: The Importance of Family-School-Community Collaborations," *School Community Journal* 27, no. 1 (2017): 149.

30. Josiane Hudicourt-Barnes, "The Use of Argumentation in Haitian Cre-ole Science Classrooms," *Harvard Educational Review* 73, no. 1 (2003): 73–93.

Chapter 4: TRIANGULATED IDENTITIES ACROSS BORDERS

1. C. L. R. James, *The Black Jacobins* (orig. 1938; New York: Vintage, 1963), 43.

2. Frank Moya Pons, *History of the Caribbean* (Princeton, NJ: Marcus Weiner Publishers, 2007), 69.

3. Pons, *History of the Caribbean*, 69.

4. *The Price of Sugar*, dir. Bill Haney (Uncommon Productions, 2007).

5. Frank Andre Guridy, *Forging Diaspora: Afro-Cubans and African Americans in a World of Empire and Jim Crow* (Chapel Hill: University of North Carolina Press, 2010).

6. Christina A. Sue, *Land of the Cosmic Race: Race Mixture, Racism, and Blackness in Mexico* (London: Oxford University Press, 2013), 7.

7. Thomas Madiou, *Histoire D'Haïti: Tome I, 1492–1799* (orig. 1847; Port-au-Prince: Éditions Henri Deschamps, 1989).

8. David Nicholls, *From Dessalines to Duvalier: Race, Colour and National Independence in Haiti*, Warwick University Caribbean Studies (Basingstoke, UK: Macmillan Caribbean, 1988), 142.

9. Robert May, *The Southern Dream of a Caribbean Empire, 1854–1861* (Gainesville: University Press of Florida, 2002), 33.

10. May, *The Southern Dream of a Caribbean Empire*, 35.

11. May, *The Southern Dream of a Caribbean Empire*, 176.

12. Silvio Torres-Saillant, *Introduction to Dominican Blackness* (New York: CUNY Dominican Studies Institute, 2010), 5.

13. Silvio Torres-Saillant, *Introduction to Dominican Blackness*, 5–6.

14. Lucia Newman, "Race and Racism in Latin America: Skin Color in the Dominican Republic," Al Jazeera, July 2008, https://www.youtube.com/watch?v=zubBxJsqdlI.

15. Michelle Wucker, *Why the Cocks Fight: Dominicans, Haitians, and the Struggle for Hispaniola* (New York: Hill and Wang, 1999), 49.

16. Kimberlé Crenshaw, "Race, Reform, and Retrenchment: Transformation and Legitimation in Antidiscrimination Law," in *Critical Race Theory*, ed. Kimberlé Crenshaw, Neil Gotanda, Gary Peller, Kendall Thomas (New York: New Press, 1996), 107.

17. Martin Luther King Jr., *Stride Toward Freedom* (San Francisco: Harper San Francisco, 1958), 194.

18. Clayton Rosa, "Caught in Between: A Dominican Journey into Race," June 2013, http://www.cimamag.com/caught-in-between-a-dominicanos-journey-into-race.

19. Rosa, "Caught in Between."

20. Wendy Roth, *Race Migrations: Latinos and Cultural Transformations of Race* (Stanford, CA: Stanford University Press, 2012), 175.

21. Biany Pérez, on "Black in the Dominican Republic: Denying Blackness," hosted by Marc Lamont Hill, Huffington Post Live, June 13, 2014, http://live.huffingtonpost.com/r/segment/dominican-black -ancestry-africa-denial—latin-america/5390c27802a760d1de00037e.

22. Steven Gregory, *The Devil Behind the Mirror* (Berkeley: University of California Press, 2007), 45.

23. Robin Derby, on "Black in the Dominican Republic."

Patrick Sylvain is a Haitian-American educator, poet, writer, and social and literary critic who has published widely on Haitian diaspora culture, politics, language, and religion. He is the author of several poetry books in English and Haitian. His poems have been nominated for the prestigious Pushcart Prize, and he is widely published in several anthologies and academic journals. Sylvain has degrees from the University of Massachusetts (BA), Harvard University (EdM), and Boston University (MFA). Sylvain is a lecturer in Brown University's Africana Studies Department as well as in Brandeis University's AAAS Department, where he is completing his PhD in English.

Jalene Tamerat is a leader in K–12 education whose work focuses on the preparation of teachers who are able to respond to the instructional and civic needs of diverse urban youth. She began her career in education in 2003 as a classroom teacher in the Boston Public Schools and has most recently served as the dean of a Boston-area residency and master's program for aspiring teachers.

Marie Lily Cerat has worked in the K–16 New York public education system as a classroom teacher, staff developer, and college teacher for over twenty years. Her work examines the effects of the exclusion of Haitian language and culture in the education of Haitian learners and has been published in *Rethinking Schools*, the *Journal of Haitian Studies*, and the *International Journal of the Sociology of Language*, among other publications.